82132

1973

Singer, Dorothy G.

Teaching televi-
sion

TEACHING TELEVISION

TEACHING TELEVISION

How to use TV to your child's advantage

Dorothy G. Singer, Ed.D.
Jerome L. Singer, Ph.D.
Diana M. Zuckerman, Ph.D.

The Dial Press New York

Published by
The Dial Press
1 Dag Hammarskjold Plaza
New York, New York 10017

Manufactured in the United States of America

First printing

Original art by Anne G. Chesnut

Library of Congress Cataloging in Publication Data

Singer, Dorothy G
   Teaching television.

   Bibliography: p.
   Includes index.
   1. Children and television. 2. Television in preschool education—United States. I. Singer, Jerome L., joint author. II. Zuckerman, Diana M., joint author.
III. Title.
HQ784.T4S54   372.13'358   80-20775
ISBN 0-8037-8515-1

To the elementary school children in
Orange, Connecticut

CONTENTS

Preface   ix
ONE   The Challenges of Television   3
TWO   Constructive Possibilities of Tele-
             vision   18
THREE   Parents' Questions about TV:
             Some Answers   36
FOUR   When You Watch and What You
             Watch   46
FIVE   How Television Works   62
SIX   TV Magic: Effects and Special
             Effects   73
SEVEN   Real and Pretend on TV   89
EIGHT   Characters We Love and Hate:
             Learning   about   Ourselves
             through People We Meet on TV   110
NINE   TV Is Only Part of the Picture   122
TEN   Violence and Action on TV   135
ELEVEN   Commercials and the Television
             Business   156
TWELVE   You and TV: Who's in Charge   172
Appendix   Sources for Television-Related
             Materials   189
References   193
Index   203

PREFACE

Television has become increasingly important in children's lives. The average elementary school-aged child spends as much time watching television each day (five hours) as he or she spends in school. Even though some children spend considerably less time watching TV, the time they do spend is time they will not be using for reading books, playing with friends, pursuing hobbies, talking with family members, and other such important activities.

Television is here to stay, and although parents sometimes worry about their children's viewing habits, most parents feel unable or unwilling to limit effectively children's television viewing. The purpose of this book is to encourage parents to use television programs to stimulate their children's learning and creativity, and to help parents teach their children to be more selective television consumers. The activities are designed to be used with the TV programs that the children are already watching, and to make sure that the children understand program content as well as the differences between reality and fantasy on television. In addition, children's natural interest in television programs is used as a motivating factor to teach them critical-thinking skills, reading and writing skills, and to encourage creativity.

This book is not intended to increase children's television viewing, but instead to help children get the most out of the programs they are already watching. Our intent is to stimulate more active participation between parent and child, and to counteract the passive-TV-viewing syndrome. We also offer guidelines for parents who want to limit a child's viewing, and who want to help their children develop better television-viewing habits.

There are some parents who feel it is best for children not to see television at all until they are in elementary school and already reading. We are inclined to agree, yet most families are not prepared to implement such a drastic policy. In the following pages, therefore, we have tried to develop exercises for learning about television, a set of methods and guidelines for educating parents about some of the problems and constructive possibilities of the television medium, and information on how to get the most from television. If we can't make the television sets go away, we will have to learn to integrate them into our homes in a way that is consistent with the values *we* respect and consistent with what seems to make good sense for education.

The materials for this book were developed under the auspices of the Yale University Family Research and Consultation Center. Support for this project came in the form of a grant from the American Broadcasting Companies, Inc. Details of the research project and the development of material presented in this book are, however, solely the responsibility of the authors. No attempt was made by the ABC Network in any way to influence our research methodology or the content of the lessons.

The focus of the project was upon shifting the emphasis in children's use of the medium from a passive toward a more active, potentially adaptive orientation. The study involved the preparation of a module including eight lessons which could ultimately become part of a regular elementary school social studies curriculum.

Teachers received training in how to present materials in class. Parents attended workshops where they received information concerning ways in which they could share in making the natural television-viewing experience a more constructive one for their children.

The study focused on children in third, fourth, and fifth grades of elementary school (eight- , nine- , and ten-year-olds). The reasons for the initial emphasis on this group were as follows:

- Statistical analyses suggest that children in this age-group are among the heaviest television viewers—about 4½ hours per day.
- Recent reviews of available research literature suggest that these years just before onset of adolescence are particularly important for formulation of adult media habits, including use of magazines, newspapers, and television.
- Because preadolescent years are the "locus for change," this age-group would be particularly suited for attempts by parents and teachers to exert their influence in regard to use of television. Evidence suggests that parental communication and teacher modeling, rather than peer pressures, are still most important at this period.
- Reading emerges as a critical skill in this age-group and is needed for all school subject matter. Because of the children's natural interest in TV, their responsiveness to that medium might be used to enhance cognitive and social skills needed in reading.
- The largest group of referrals to school psychologists for learning problems, restless behavior, and reading remediation falls within the third to fifth grades and suggests, therefore, that this age-group could benefit from intervention strategies designed to enhance learning skills and to reduce potential negative effects of excessive TV viewing or dependence.

• There is still some variability among these children in terms of their understanding of what is reality and what is fantasy. Thus, this group, in a transitional period of cognitive growth, may need help in developing reasoning and logical-thinking skills.

Details and results of the study will be presented in Chapter 2. See the References list for journal articles pertaining to this project.

We want to thank our staff at the Yale University Family Television Research and Consultation Center for their devotion and skill in developing the materials: Arthur Greenwald, Roseann Hirshman, Jill Garnett, Richard Stoving. Paul Christoph helped with statistical design. Karen Banta and Charlotte Shah were our excellent secretaries. Roseann Hirshman, Carol Wiedeman and Mary Plate did the preliminary illustrations and deserve credit for their efforts. Additional thanks goes to Richard Gerrig for help with references and with the many mechanical aspects of getting the manuscript ready.

We want to thank the American Broadcasting Companies, Inc., for their financial support, and especially Melvin Goldberg, Director of Research, and Pamela Warford, Director of Community Relations. We also thank Tom Madden, formerly of ABC, who was encouraging and supportive of our initial proposal. Thank you, Virginia Hurd, for the excellent job in typing the manuscript and for helping us keep our balance. Thanks to Bruce Singer for his suggestions and comments. We owe a special debt to Lawrence Michelotti and Andrew Himmel for their excellent editorial comments and encouragement.

Finally, thanks to the Orange Schools and their teachers for their willingness to participate in the study. A special thanks to Dr. Vincent Cibbarelli, superintendent of Orange Elementary Schools, for permitting us to proceed.

Particular thanks and appreciation to Diana M. Zuckerman for her care in directing the project.

Dorothy G. Singer
Jerome L. Singer
Co-Directors
Family Television Research and Consultation Center
New Haven, January 1980

TEACHING TELEVISION

ONE

THE CHALLENGES OF TELEVISION

Children today are growing up in an environment that never existed before in human experience. Aside from family, friends, and the sights, smells, and noises of their homes, children today grow up with a little box which provides them with a vast array of sights and sounds: funny cartoon animals falling apart and being miraculously put together, gangsters shooting down their victims with machine guns, or cars pursuing each other down narrow roads, chorus girls kicking up their legs, and incessant interruptions by commercials in which humorous and lively figures dangle attractive candy bars or toys in front of children's eyes. That was a long sentence, but we used it on purpose. We wanted to capture the quality of the experience of a child who begins looking at the television set somewhere between one and two years of age and then continues watching it daily for as much as four or five hours as he or she grows up.

The evidence is pretty clear on the point of the child's exposure to television. More than 96 percent of American families own at least one television set, according to the 1970 census report, and many own two or three. In a certain sense then the television set can

be viewed, as we have put it elsewhere, as "a member of the family." It is a major source of input of verbal and visual stimulation for the growing child, and we must begin to take serious account of its impact.

SOME COGNITIVE PROPERTIES OF THE TELEVISION MEDIUM

While it is likely that movies have a greater impact than television, very young children rarely go to the cinema. Instead, they are exposed daily, as we have suggested, to large amounts of highly emotional material on the TV set.

Aside from the obvious characteristics of television— its availability in the home, its use of picture and sound, and its entertainment, information, and social value— television has certain properties that distinguish it from other communication media. They are:

- *Attention demand*—the continuous movement on the screen that evokes first an "orienting response" and then as movements become rapid and music louder, a general activation of the nervous system.
- *Brevity of sequences*—the brief interactions among people, brief portrayals of events, brief commercials (from 15 to 60 seconds long).
- *Interference effects*—the rapid succession of material that possibly interferes with the child's rehearsal and assimilation of new material.
- *Complexity of presentation*—the presentation of material to several senses at once—sight, sound, and printed words, especially in the commercial.

- *Visual orientation*—Television is by its very nature concrete, oriented toward visual imagery, minimizing detailed attention to the other sources of input of information.
- *Emotional range*—The vividness of the action presented is greater than on other media.

In addition to these features there are the use of slow motion or speeded motion, the juxtaposition of scenes or split-screen techniques whereby two pictures are placed side by side on the same screen, the use of subliminal techniques which allow two scenes to be viewed simultaneously (often used in dream sequences), and special camera effects such as zooming in (the enlargement of a character or object), making objects appear small or making them gradually grow before your eyes, the production of magical effects involving distortions, changes in figure and ground, ripple effects of words or scenes, and, of course, the use of lighting and background music to create illusion. We are just beginning to see research appearing on whether these effects enhance or confuse a child's imagination and capacity to understand.

PROBLEMS PRESENTED BY THE TELEVISION

Consider the problem, then, of understanding what is going on in the young child's mind. Miniature figures dance about on the screen; characters make statements which are quickly interrupted by new characters or changes in time or location. These rapid changes undoubtedly hold the child's attention on the screen, but one might argue that they do so at the cost of allowing the child an opportunity to *process* this material effectively. In other words, when subjected to very rapid presentations of novel material, the child lacks the time to replay this material mentally in what psychologists call the "echo box" of the short-term-memory system. After material is repeated in short-term memory, it can then be transferred to the brain's longer-term-memory system, from which it can later be retrieved as we need it.

The situation is not unlike one you might recognize yourself: coming into a party where the host introduces you rapidly to a whole series of people whom you have never met before. Naturally enough, you remember few names, if any. Television has a similar impact on young children. Its very liveliness holds their attention, arouses them, and may make them laugh, but they may have trouble remembering much of what they have seen afterward. There is a real danger that the rapidity of presentation may create "mindless" watching, so that by the end of the program there is little genuine comprehension of what has been watched, and often scarcely any memory. The once popular show, *Laugh-In*, provides a good example. Its pace was extremely rapid, jokes and visual effects piled with tremendous speed upon each other, coming at one from different angles of the screen. One laughed continuously throughout the show, but at the end it was almost impossible to recall a single joke.

We don't wish to minimize the importance television may have for some people as a distraction. We often

watch it to avoid thinking about the many pressing
unfinished tasks of our daily life. Old people certainly
find that it provides them with "company" to help
them deal with loneliness. Nevertheless, if television's
rapid-fire presentation of images serves to preclude
comprehension and recall, we wonder about its value.

At first one might think that television, with so much
new vocabulary and so many new sights being presented to the child, would be on the whole an enriching
experience. We must remember, however, that children are not miniature adults. When they watch a television program, they are comprehending the material
on a different level from their parents'. Children below
the age of seven view the world illogically, or in what
Jean Piaget, the eminent Swiss psychologist, calls "preoperational thought." They have difficulty separating
reality from fantasy; they believe in animism, or the
notion that inanimate objects, such as a teddy bear, can
talk. They believe that human beings created lakes,
mountains, sun, moon; they believe in magical thinking, and through their chants of "rain, rain go away"
hope to control the elements. Their concepts of space
and time are distorted. For example, a young child may
believe that someone who lives 300 miles away is actually closer than someone who lives 60 miles away. If the
trip to the farther point is made by plane it is *shorter*
in time than the trip to the nearer point when one
travels by car. Young children believe taller people are
older than shorter people. Children in the pre-opera-
tional stage think concretely; therefore metaphors and
similes are difficult for them to understand. Words have
literal meanings for them—the North Pole is a long

stick, "tied up at work" conjures up a picture of Daddy tied to his chair, and "he's lost his marbles" might make a youngster search on the floor.

Children listen to words spoken on television, but like Mork, they may be confused, misinterpret meanings, or perhaps even become frightened or upset at what they hear.

Certainly it is true that television creates a uniformity of experience across grossly different cultural groups within the country and, indeed, internationally. Almost everyone in America now knows how to sing the McDonald's hamburger jingle. To what extent, however, is the heavy visual emphasis of the medium affecting growing girls and boys? Important research by Sandra Witelson suggests that girls are less differentiated than boys in right- and left-brain functioning. This means that they can use more of their brain for dealing with both verbal and spatial, or imagery, material. Educators know that boys in the first seven or eight years of life are much more likely to have language difficulties than girls; the ratio is almost ten to one. The fact is that boys are heavier television viewers than girls and are thus more exposed to visually oriented material in which the verbal component is presented at extremely rapid rates. It is quite possible that this heavy visual emphasis creates further difficulties for a boy's ability to label verbally the images that are presented. In our own research we did find advantages for the girls in kindergarten in language usage, even though they watched as much television as the boys.

It is also apparent from various research studies that children who watch a great deal of television are not engaging in an active verbal interchange, an important part of how one learns to use language effectively. In a study Eva Essa found that kindergarten-aged children, even when they were watching with their mothers, did not engage in much talk with the parents and simply regarded the set passively. Children who were heavy viewers did not show much play at other times, while children who were light viewers showed much more general interaction with their mothers and also more play with toys. In another study Elizabeth Susman found that some of the special effects, such as zooming of the camera, tended to interfere with children's capacity to attend to the nature of the material being presented. Although for adults this so-called zoom effect may certainly focus attention, kindergarten-aged children are not able to benefit from this special effect and, if anything, seem to be confused by it.

Unusual circumstances in Canada made it possible to compare three cities in which there were drastic differences in the availability of television. In one city, television had just been introduced for the first time. Linda Harrison, who carried out research on these cities, found that children, once having been exposed to television for a period of at least two years, showed a reduction in performance on a test where they were asked to name as many possible uses for common objects as they could. This drop indicated less creativity or original thinking by children who had now been watching TV regularly compared with the pre-television level.

The general trend of recent research seems to suggest that television may cause difficulties for children in developing the more active aspects of memory, in developing social interchange with parents (which enhances language use), and in developing an attitude of playfulness and imaginativeness. In an important project Robert Hornik studied groups of children in El Salvador who were for the first time being exposed to television. He found strong evidence that reading improvement was *slowest* in children who now had a TV set, and that there was even some evidence that television interfered with general learning and reading ability. Here the simple distracting quality of the television set, interfering with the amount of time necessary to practice reading, was undoubtedly a factor. In our own research we found that children who were heavy TV viewers, and particularly viewers of "action" shows, had special difficulty in language development and in imaginative play. These children were also more aggressive and more likely to have difficulties in their day-to-day behavior in kindergarten.

In a more recent study with over 200 working-class families, we found that heavy *Sesame Street* viewers tended to be among our most aggressive children in the nursery schools. It is possible that the fast pacing and short segments, ranging from about ten seconds to a minute and a half, may have been causing an arousal effect, and that the children's inability to process all the material properly causes their disquietude, restlessness, and increased likelihood of aggressive behavior in their play.

Another experimental study we carried out compared the effect of watching a slow-paced show, *Mister Rogers' Neighborhood*, with that of watching the relatively rapid-paced children's show *Sesame Street*.

While the brighter young girls were able to learn more of the material seen on *Sesame Street*, it turned out that the less intelligent boys and less imaginative children did somewhat better with the slower-paced *Mister Rogers'*. In a book, *"Sesame Street" Revisited*, Thomas D. Cook and his colleagues reported that middle-class children actually learned more from *Sesame Street* than lower-class children, because they were encouraged to watch the program by their parents. These parents may also have been more active in reinforcing ideas from *Sesame Street* with their children than parents in lower socioeconomic groups. If we are to avoid any kind of knowledge gap, we must provide as wide a variety of television formats as possible so that children from all backgrounds can profit from viewing. We must also clearly encourage parents to interact with their children as they watch television.

There are two more special problems about television viewing that we should like to mention. One is the fact that in general the pacing of programs may prevent a child from practicing his own imagery and trying out in play and thought some of the new material he has observed. In effect, the TV format trains one simply to watch the set and to be satisfied with that.

We found in our own research that with the *Mister Rogers'* program, in which great emphasis was placed on repetition of words, on careful phrasing, on encouragement of imagination and the child's "talking back" to the set, children were able to play more imaginatively than when they watched other kinds of television fare. Having an adult available who would encourage imaginativeness was quite important as well.

Television, according to W. Andrew Collins, has also created difficulties for kindergartners in understanding causal sequences. That is, children who saw aggressive acts could rarely comprehend the notion of whether the act was motivated by good or bad intentions. They simply remembered the fact of the aggression. And, indeed, there is increasing evidence from a variety of research studies which suggest that the excitement of the aggression is imitated in many different ways by the children. Our own research suggests that kindergarten children who had displayed aggressive behavior for over a year were also more likely to have watched programs with arousing content, such as game shows in which the winners leap up and down screaming hysterically.

One final point: The television set keeps moving. It is a medium that is controlled externally. Information flashes by and the child cannot go back over it. There is no sense of control over the medium except to shut it off. One can perhaps envision a time when the widespread availability of video cassettes or cable-television techniques in which hand switches are employed might give one at least some sense of input into what appears on the screen. But today, material does not stay within the control of the individual. Television is not like reading, for example, where one has the possibility of self-pacing. With a book, one can go back and forth with a text and read it again and again until the material is grasped more firmly. To some degree one has a sense of control over the reading process. At the same time there exists the possibility of stopping, of elaborating more fully upon one's visual or auditory images in connection with the material, and thus increasing the possibility of storing the materials in the brain in an efficient fashion. Clearly this is a very distinct process from what goes on in the television-viewing situation.

It might seem unlikely that one can develop imagery as vivid and rich from reading as one can from the immediacy of a television presentation. Nevertheless, the images that have been developed while reading have been worked at and are more clearly one's own. There can be far greater richness and subtlety of detail in the act of reading than in watching a TV or even a film presentation; this is why people who have "read the book" are so often disappointed by the movie.

A brief word may be said here about radio. Some of us who grew up in the era of radio stories may still recall the vividness with which we created our own visual images to go along with the dialogue we heard from the set. One could move around the room, even occasionally read while listening to the radio and still process a good deal of the material. It thus demanded less attention than a TV set and allowed more of what we would call "channel space" for private processing and the development of private images. It might be worth seeing, through experimental methods, whether we can compare for children or adults the effects on learning and imagination of television viewing, reading, or radio listening, and perhaps even determine which combination is most efficient for adaptive cognitive functions in the growing child.

Since reading is a basic skill for effective functioning in our modern society, we have to be concerned about the possibility that heavy television viewing, and par-

ticularly viewing under circumstances which may preclude the development of imagination, may also interfere with the child's development of reading skills.
We've already mentioned the important work of Hornik which suggests that children who have begun to
watch television regularly are distracted from reading
and show slower growth of reading and other kinds of
intellectual capacities. It is also possible that a well-
developed imagination prepares the child for general
intellectual growth. Certainly we know that training in
play has been shown (by Kenneth Rubin, Robert Fink,
and Claire Golomb) to increase the very young child's
capacity to recognize that quantity and volume remain
constant. Preschool children are more influenced by
perception than by logical reasoning. They learn
through experience, for example, that four ounces of
water in a small, wide glass still remains four ounces of
water when poured into a tall, thin glass, even though
the water rises to the top and looks like more. Play
training facilitates this.

It may sound as if television is an enemy and that we
are sounding a call to arms for the abolition of television, as in Marie Winn's book *The Plug-In Drug*. In one
of our research studies we attempted to train parents
to control and severely limit children's TV viewing.
This turned out to be very difficult to do. Parents like
television themselves, and they also find it an extremely
convenient baby-sitter. In fact, parents from the poorer
inner-city neighborhoods often say that they would
rather have their children home watching television
than out in the streets confronting various dangers.
Rather than abolish television, we should find ways of

harnessing its tremendous power in the direction of more effective education for children.

We feel that there ought to be better material available for children to watch. In the United States there are very very few programs available to kindergarten-aged children or even children below the age of twelve that are seriously designed to be both entertaining and educational, promoting intellectual growth and also a sense of cooperation and positive social attitudes. We would like to see television producers provide more material with pacing that is appropriate for children to comprehend and with much more conscious effort to communicate directly with the younger children.

We are also concerned about possibilities of introducing training materials in the classroom, even as early as the kindergarten level, which will alert children to the ways they can actually draw materials from television for their own cognitive growth. The material in this book was developed from the special lessons taught to children in the upper grades on the nature of the television medium itself. Thus we hope to inform children about how the set works, how special effects are obtained, the nature of television commercials, the nature of violence, reality and fantasy, stereotypes, etc.

In effect, our position is that the television medium can be a great advantage for the growing child and a stimulant for imagination if material is presented in a format that is suitable for the child. Our school lessons make a special point of encouraging imaginativeness and, for the older children, include exercises that involve practice in reading and writing with ideas drawn from television.

Ultimately, of course, the adults in the child's life, the parent and the teacher, have the most to contribute in stimulating the child's imagination and encouraging an atmosphere that will lead on the one hand to a willingness and interest in reading, and on the other to a discriminating and moderate approach to television viewing. One of our favorite images of the joys of childrearing is the scene of the father or mother or grandparent telling a tale or reading from a book to a wide-eyed, eager child. Certainly, no electronic device can ever substitute for the warmth of interchange between a loving adult and a child at storytelling time; nevertheless, in the following chapters we hope to show that television can be used creatively toward constructive ends.

TWO

CONSTRUCTIVE POSSIBILITIES OF TELEVISION

Sol Levine of Highland Park, Ill., estimates that he is saving the nation one barrel of crude oil a year by having his children pedal a bike-generator he invented to power their television set.

"I'd come home and find my two kids immobilized in front of their set and I figured they should be doing something if they wanted to watch it," says Levine, president of an ecology center for saving energy. "I took their bicycle, made a stand for it in the TV room, hooked it to a car generator and a 12-volt battery. Now they can feed their television habit with their own energy." Levine says the pedal power can work only on a set about the size used by Bennet, 15, and Linda, 12—a black-and-white portable with a 12-inch screen. "I pedal with them sometimes to watch the late news," Levine says. "It's good exercise. My wife used to join us pedaling through programs, but now she regards it mainly as exercise. When the kids are at school, she will do some pedaling in the afternoon and help charge the battery."

On a busy TV night, Levine and the children take turns pedaling, storing electricity for five-minute recesses. "We usually take a break during commercials."

—Quoted in *Newsday, The Long Island Newspaper*

Mr. Levine is one parent who is aware of television's power over his children. The average number of hours spent viewing television varies from about 3 hours a day for preschoolers to 5 hours a day for elementary school-aged children. We also know that poor and black children spend even more time—approximately 5½ to 6 hours per day—before the television set. In our own studies at the Yale Family Television Research and Consultation Center, we have found that both middle-class and lower-class children average about 22 to 23 hours per week, and for our middle-class sample the range of viewing per week was from 1 to 72 hours. Obviously, television is playing an important part in children's lives; for a large segment of the school-aged population, more time is spent in front of the screen than in school.

Our studies (one begun in 1976, with a sample of 140 middle-class children, and a current study with 200 working-class families that we have just completed) support findings concerning the deleterious effect of TV on children. Children who are heavy television viewers and who are the most aggressive in our samples watch action-detective shows, cartoons, news, and game shows. We find that both the hours spent in front of television and program content are significant. For example, heavy viewers of educational programs do not exhibit as much aggressive behavior as viewers of action-detective shows.

In addition to the television viewing patterns of children, family interaction and behavior also influence a child's capacity for aggression. We found that an aggressive child is more likely to be part of a family that uses television as its main socializing force. They spend little time visiting zoos, parks, relatives, or libraries. The focus of entertainment is television. Meals are even spent in front of the set, inhibiting communication. Thus, there is little to protect the child against the powerful effect of the television characters—especially those who present models for aggression and violence. The most shocking finding is that in these homes the child controls the set and stays up late viewing with his or her family.

The field work of Leon Eron, our work at the Yale TV Research Center, studies such as those by William Belson, Lynette Friedrich, and Aletha Stein, and the classic laboratory studies of Albert Bandura and his co-workers all have demonstrated the effects of watching aggressive adults on children's subsequent behavior. Indeed, there is an impressive body of literature that deals with the negative effects of television, but there are constructive projects that are taking place both in the home and in the classroom that could lead to more effective uses.

Our approach at the Yale Family Television Research and Consultation Center has been to focus on the effects of TV on children and to develop ideas for positive uses of television. We are interested in television's impact on a child's imagination, aggression, and language development, and consequently have designed most of our projects so that we can observe children during their free play in nursery schools and day-care centers. We have also carried out studies involving older children and have gone into elementary schools to gather data. Some of our projects have involved extensive family interviews as well. None of our work thus far has followed a laboratory model, but rather involves field studies covering several months to approximately three years. We are attempting in two major studies to follow young children from nursery school through their early school years to see if television has a long-range impact on their imagination, language, and development of reading skills. One unique aspect of our work is the careful record-keeping by parents of their children's television habits during each experiment. Our workshops have also given us the opportunity to offer parents child-rearing information as well as positive ways to use television. We will briefly summarize the results of some of the projects we have developed.

EFFECTS OF TELEVISION ON PRESCHOOLERS, AND THE DEVELOPMENT OF LESSON PLANS BASED ON TELEVISION FOR USE IN NURSERY SCHOOLS AND DAY-CARE CENTERS

The aims of this study were twofold: (1) to study the effects of television on 200 lower-class preschoolers and (2) to see if using particular ideas from television programs and forming them into lessons could increase a child's imagination, social skills (sharing, cooperation, turn-taking) and cognitive skills (counting, recognizing shapes, forms, colors, and categorizing similar objects). The lessons were extensions of an idea or concept presented on a particular program and taught by the teacher in the nursery school. Since research indicates that children from poorer families are among the heaviest television viewers, we felt that we might be able to help these children become more active viewers when they did watch television. Using only two- or three-minute television segments from educational shows, we were able to reinforce concepts through active classroom discussion and participation. Over a year's time, using varying conditions, we were able to determine the usefulness of adult mediation with television programs. One group of children simply followed the standard nursery school curriculum; one group used our special materials; and the last group used television plus the special materials. This last group made more overall developmental gains than the other two. Half of the parents in each group attended workshops during the year.

Results indicate that these preschoolers were watching television from three to four hours daily, with a sizeable minority watching from five to six hours daily. We also found that behaviors such as imagination, cooperation, leadership, and positive emotionality were linked together. Our data indicate that by three or four years of age children show considerable consistency in their play patterns and TV-viewing styles, suggesting that personality and social behaviors are fairly well established by these ages. Of special interest is the evidence that imaginative play is strongly linked with cooperative behavior and is not characteristic of the isolated or lonely child. Our data suggest that children who get into more difficulties at school and show less mature group behavior are among our heavier viewers, watch *more* action-adventure (violent) programming, and are *less* likely to be watching prosocial programs on public television, such as *Mister Rogers' Neighborhood.*

A major finding of our data indicates a link between aggressive behavior and the viewing of *Sesame Street* and action-adventure programming. This confirms results obtained earlier in our work with middle-class preschoolers. In our present sample these findings are especially characteristic of lower-IQ, nonwhite boys. Nevertheless, at the end of the year, we found that aggression in school, lack of persistence, high level of motor activity, and the viewing of action-adventure programs, regardless of IQ or race, were clearly linked.

Finally, in the condition where children received TV plus the teacher's reinforcement of the lesson, and especially when parents of these children came to workshops, children showed gains in imagination, interaction with peers, cooperation with peers, leadership, and a reduction of aggression in the classroom.

USING TELEVISION IN NURSERY SCHOOLS WITH MIDDLE-CLASS CHILDREN

In this study we attempted to assess a new television program about a bear to see if a format involving education as well as entertainment could benefit 60 nursery school children. We used two different schools for this project, both middle class, in different sections of Connecticut. One group of children, the control group, watched videotapes of children's stories which were neutral in social content. Another group watched the special "bear" program, and a third group watched the special "bear" program but had a follow-up discussion with activities directed by the teacher.

Results indicate that the children who watched the special program and had a follow-up lesson with the teacher significantly increased their knowledge of words and ideas related to the program content, suggesting that good programming is more effective with adult interaction.

A STUDY TO DETERMINE TELEVISION'S EFFECTS ON FRIENDSHIP PATTERNS, COOPERATION, AND MORAL DEVELOPMENT

This study was carried out in a Connecticut town with 78 children in third grade and 93 fifth graders to see if viewing television under various conditions could lead to changes in attitudes toward friends and parents, and to changes in moral reasoning.

Episodes from *Fables of the Green Forest* and *Swiss Family Robinson* were shown to third and fifth graders respectively. Before the third-grade children were randomly assigned to one of three possible conditions, they were pretested on a measure of moral reasoning and friendship patterns. Similarly, fifth-grade children were pretested on a measure of moral reasoning and attitudes about the family before they were randomly assigned to the three conditions.

In one condition, after each program (third graders viewing *Fables* and fifth graders viewing *Swiss Family Robinson*) a teacher led a discussion based on some situation in the program that dealt with prosocial content. In the other condition the children saw each program, but no discussion followed. In a third condition children viewed neutral films such as nature programs.

Parents kept records of the children's television viewing patterns one week before the experiment and one week after the experiment. Children were post-tested twice—immediately after the two weeks of the film condition and three months later—to determine whether effects would continue. Results indicated that the fifth-grade children did not exhibit a shift in their *stage* of moral reasoning. However, children in the Teacher Lesson group showed less of a "help-only-those-who-help-you" attitude and were also less inclined to be selfish. There were also significant changes found regarding being seen as "nice" as justification for making a decision. Fifth graders appeared less negative about their families and accepted a non-sex-stereotyped concept about parent-child interactions. They also had a more positive attitude concerning family interaction in general.

Third graders displayed less concern with the expectations of authority prior to making a decision. The Teacher Lesson group discussed friendship in less superficial terms and stressed more personal aspects such as quality of interaction and discussion of home and personal problems.

COULD SPECIAL PROGRAMS DESIGNED FOR YOUNG
PEOPLE STIMULATE DISCUSSION BETWEEN PARENT
AND CHILD?

We were curious to see if a group of 21 teenagers could express feelings about issues raised in a program designed specifically for them. Six television programs were selected for the study, which was conducted over a six-month period. The children viewed the tapes in a group, without parents present, and then discussed the programs with two trained leaders. The programs dealt with such topics as death, stealing, prejudice toward blacks, feelings of isolation, need for trust, and how young people learn to draw on their own resources in order to survive a blizzard.

Results indicated that the young people significantly increased their communication with their parents. We also found increased concentration, more time spent on homework, and less time spent watching television. The control group who watched the programs over the same period, with their parents present, made no significant changes on the measures used. Their parents may have inhibited discussion.

TEACHING ELEMENTARY SCHOOL CHILDREN TO
BECOME CRITICAL CONSUMERS OF TELEVISION

The project most important to this book is a study we designed to teach elementary school children how to be more discriminating television viewers. We developed an eight-lesson curriculum that was used for four weeks at two schools in Orange, Connecticut, a suburb of New Haven. Each lesson discussed an aspect of television aimed at increasing children's understanding of TV and developing a more critical approach to TV viewing.

The major goals of the lessons were as follows:

1. To understand the different types of television programs, such as news, documentaries, variety, game shows, situation comedies, and drama
2. To understand that programs are created by writers, producers, and directors, and utilize actors and actresses, as well as scenery and props
3. To understand the simple electronics of television
4. To learn what aspects of a program are real, and how fantasy is created on programs or commercials by using camera techniques and special effects
5. To learn about commercials, their purpose, and what kinds there are, such as public service or political announcements
6. To understand how television influences our feelings, ideas, self-concept, and identification
7. To become aware of television as a source of information about other people, countries, and occupations; and how politics and stereotypes are presented
8. To examine violence on television with a view toward taking out false glamour. To become aware that we rarely see someone recovering from an act of violence on TV, or see the aggressor punished
9. To encourage children to be aware of what they watch and how they can control their viewing habits, and of how they can influence networks, producers, and local TV stations
10. To use these lessons within a language arts curriculum so that children could gain experience in using correct grammar and spelling, writing letters, abstracting ideas,

critical thinking, using language effectively, oral discussion, and reading

We designed each lesson to run about 40 to 50 minutes. Included were activities for classroom and homework, and the lessons encompassed reading, writing, and critical-thinking skills.

The teacher introduced the lesson using a discussion guide that we had prepared. For example, in dealing with the lesson on violence and aggression, the children were asked to name any show they had seen the previous week that had aggression in it. These were listed on the blackboard. Children were asked to define aggression and to make distinctions between physical and verbal aggression. They talked about the difference between aggression and assertiveness, and the meaning of violence. A ten-minute videotape was shown, followed by discussion exploring the causes and effects of violent acts. Did they see the victim suffer? Did they see punishment meted out on the TV screen? Teachers asked whether or not anyone had ever imitated an aggressive act following a show. In one homework assignment, for example, children were asked to keep track of aggressive acts in a cartoon or dramatic program that they had recently watched. All lessons followed a discussion-activity format.

Sitting in on the lessons was an exciting experience for us. Since television is so much a part of a child's life, it serves as a common denominator with respect to shared experiences. The children knew the characters on the TV tapes we used, and responded to them with enthusiasm. The discussions concerning the lessons on aggression and violence were the most moving. For example when the teacher asked a class of third graders who they liked on TV, many boys said The Hulk. When questioned about this preference, they replied, "He's big," "strong," "powerful," "He can do anything." But when the teacher asked if The Hulk was happy, the class responded with such answers as "No, he has a demon inside of him," "It's not good to be out of control," "He never knows when he'll become a different person." The children also reported on how they sometimes imitated aggressive acts, especially after viewing programs like *CHiPs* or *Baretta*. Many of the children said they "really didn't feel good" when they watched violence on TV.

In order to evaluate whether the children learned what they had been taught in the lessons, we tested them before and after the four-week curriculum. We compared their test scores with those of children in another school who took the same tests but did not receive the curriculum that we developed.

Our comparisons of the test scores demonstrated that children made gains in defining lesson-related words such as *audio, fiction, prop,* and *aggression.* They also learned to identify videotaped examples of special effects, and to describe how camera techniques and effects distort reality in programs and commercials. In addition, they learned to better differentiate between real people, realistic characters, and fantasy characters. Three months after the lessons were completed, the children still remembered the information they had learned. Children were also able to answer questions relating to examples *not* previously taught in the lessons.

TELEVISION VIEWING HABITS AND FAMILY BACKGROUND

We also wanted to learn more about the relationship between children's TV viewing and aspects of family life. We found that the parents' viewing habits were the most important predictors of their children's. Children who spent more time watching television tended to have parents who were heavy television viewers, and were less likely to have parentally imposed limits on their TV viewing.

The children who watched many violent programs tended to have parents, especially fathers, who watched more action-violent programs. The most popular violent programs were *Battlestar Galactica, Charlie's Angels, The Incredible Hulk, Quincy, The Rockford Files, Starsky and Hutch,* and *Vega$.* Cartoons were not included in this category.

These results show us that parents' viewing habits serve as a model for "appropriate" television viewing for their children. When we asked the children how they would feel if television "disappeared from this planet tomorrow," the children who reported that they would be most upset were those whose parents watched the most television.

TELEVISION VIEWING HABITS AND TEACHER RATINGS

We were also interested to learn more about the association between children's viewing habits and their behavior in school. Teachers evaluated the chil-

dren's aggressiveness, cooperation, attentiveness, interpersonal relationships, enthusiasm, happiness, and
imagination. The viewing pattern most important in
predicting classroom behavior was watching fantasy-
violent programs such as *The Incredible Hulk, Wonder
Woman,* and *The Six Million Dollar Man.* Teachers
described children who watched more fantasy-violent
programs as less cooperative, less successful in their
relationships, less happy, and less imaginative, regardless of the children's IQ scores. Teachers rated the children who watched more cartoons as unenthusiastic
about learning. Aggressive behavior and attentiveness
in class were not related to television viewing.

TELEVISION VIEWING, READING, AND IQ

One of the most controversial issues in education is the
concern about television and reading. Will heavy television viewing affect a child's ability to read? We are
aware that children learn to read by *practicing* reading
each day, and we were curious about television's en-
croachment on reading time. We examined the reading
and IQ scores of the children in this study, as well as the
teachers' and parents' estimates of their children's
reading habits, in order to determine the relationship
between television viewing and reading.

   The children in this study watched television about
15 hours per week and are rather atypical viewers compared to the national norms of 20 to 30 hours per week
for children in this age group. The children are also
atypical in terms of IQ and reading ability, with an

average IQ of 110 and a reading score approximately one year above grade level.

Teachers kept track of the number of books the children read during a four-week period, and when one took IQ and grade level into account, the children who read more books were the ones who also watched fewer game shows and variety programs. Children who spent more time reading had higher IQ's and more highly educated fathers, and watched fewer fantasy-violent programs. It may be that children who read well, and therefore enjoy fantasy and escape through reading, rely less on television to fulfill this need. On the other hand, the poorer reader may seek his share of adventure and action by turning to television as a source.

TELEVISION VIEWING, AND RACIAL AND SEX PREJUDICE

As a part of the study, we attempted to determine whether or not television viewing was related to prejudice. We found that girls who watched more game or variety programs and reruns that present women as silly or incompetent (such as *I Love Lucy* and *The Jetsons*) were more prejudiced against girls than their classmates were. In contrast, the girls who watched more fantasy-violent programs and *fewer* other violent programs were less prejudiced against girls. The female role models in fantasy-violent programs are often competent and beautiful women (e.g., *Wonder Woman*) and are *not* the victims who are usually found in action-detective shows. Boys' sex prejudice was not related to their television habits.

Children who were the most prejudiced against black children were those who watched more violent programs (where blacks are usually portrayed in negative ways). They watched *fewer* programs with major black characters, such as *The Jeffersons* and *Diff'rent Strokes,* where blacks are portrayed more favorably.

TELEVISION VIEWING, HOBBIES, AND OTHER ACTIVITIES

Our last analysis looked at the relationship between children's TV-viewing habits and their other activities. We wanted to learn whether children who watch more television are less involved in playing with friends, pursuing hobbies, engaging in athletics, or doing things with other family members. We asked parents to describe the kinds of activities that their children regularly participated in, and asked them to estimate the amount of time they spent in these activities each week.

The children who spent the most time watching TV each week also were involved in family activities (including watching TV together) and in music and dancing. However, these children were less likely to read with their parents.

The children who were heavy viewers of violent television programs played less with friends. We don't know if this is because these children do not get along well with other children or if it is because they prefer activities such as watching violent programs to games with friends. The children who watched more fantasy-violent programs allotted less time to hobbies and less time to doing homework with their parents' help.

We were also interested in children's viewing of cartoons, situation comedies, and dramas. In each case the children who were watching TV the most were those who had fewer hobbies, played less with friends, and were less involved with athletics, religious activities, and/or music lessons. In contrast, the children who watched more sports programs allotted *more* time to athletic activities.

These results can't tell us which comes first: Does TV viewing replace other activities, or do other activities limit the amount of time children have left for TV? In either case the results suggest that children who watch less TV tend to have more interests and participate in more activities where they can learn to get along with other children, as well as family members.

This study, as well as the others described in brief, suggests that television has a place in the classroom as well as in the home if it is used with discretion. The dramatic impact of a story viewed by a group of students creates a shared emotional experience that could lead to fruitful discussion and changes in attitudes.

The use of television for cognitive, social, and emotional benefits is still in the pioneering stage. The reaction of millions of people to *Roots* and *Holocaust* suggests the positive potential of creative television programming. Too much emphasis has been placed on the negative effects of television. It's time now for educators and researchers to find ways to use this powerful medium to help influence people to live with each other in peace and mutual respect.

THREE

PARENTS' QUESTIONS ABOUT TV: SOME ANSWERS

Over the past ten years we have become increasingly aware of parental concerns regarding television. When we speak at professional conferences or parent meetings, or when we consult with mental-health workers, similar questions usually arise concerning the scheduling of appropriate programs for children, the influence of violence and aggression, the effects of cartoons and stereotypes, the effects on imagination and language, and finally the problem of what to do about commercials. In this chapter we will address those questions that are asked most frequently. Perhaps in reading this, you will recognize some of your own concerns, or indeed, you may become aware of some issues that you hadn't thought about previously.

One of the more common concerns of parents is the possibility that television could be harmful to their children's eyes. The National Society for the Prevention of Blindness offers these suggestions for television viewing:

- Focus the instrument so that the image is clear and distinct.

- The picture should be steady.
- The room should be properly lighted (not darkened), without too much contrast of light between the room and the screen. Soft, indirect lighting is best, with no light source reflected from the screen to the viewer's eyes.
- The screen should be viewed from a comfortable distance in front of the screen, not from an angle, and at eye level, not from the floor.
- Resting the eyes by looking away from the screen at frequent intervals is recommended.

Quarrels in many families revolve around program scheduling and time limits. Generally speaking, children can accept family rules if they are consistently enforced by parents and if the children are given constructive alternatives. The parents must stick to their beliefs and limit late viewing or potentially disturbing shows. For young children, the pressure of school friends should not override parents' better judgment.

When a three-year-old prefers to watch *Sesame Street* and his eight-year-old brother wants to watch his favorite show, a problem is bound to arise as to who's "boss." The decision here is an important one, for what three-year-olds watch on TV should be determined by their parents and never by older brothers or sisters. Parents can make clear for the young child that there are certain times *each* child can watch TV, and regularly limit those times so young children will grow up expecting such restrictions.

At times a baby-sitter may want to watch a program that you feel is unsuitable for your child. Be careful to let the sitter know your rules, and that you expect him or her to abide by them. Sometimes your child visits a friend and watches a program you disapprove of. You can't always be the supervisor, but hopefully, if your child truly understands your feelings about specific program viewing, he will most likely try to obey. Chances are that if you have been consistent, your child will establish viewing habits that you approve of. In general, parents should always be aware of their responsibility to know how much time the children spend with the TV and what they are watching. Parents can't assume that another family will always show good judgment. Many families don't pay attention at all to the kinds of TV their children watch and are surprised when the children have nightmares or sleeping difficulties.

Parents also ask if doing homework or eating meals in front of television is harmful. Most educators believe that even though children might get the homework done while watching TV, the division of attention prevents them from learning as effectively as when the television is turned off. Parents should establish a regular schedule to follow—an allotted time for homework and then a regular time for TV on the condition that all homework has been finished. As we pointed out earlier, watching TV reduces the amount of time needed for reading and thinking imaginatively. A regular schedule should allow time when undivided attention can be given to reading practice. This increases the likelihood that the child will develop consistently good reading habits. Except for the occasional treat, eating in front of the TV set establishes a very bad habit. It reinforces the children's dependence on TV, may lead to sloppy eating habits, and breaks down family togetherness and communication. According to research, eating while watching programs will have an even worse effect of "hooking" children on TV. A sense of family structure would be better served by keeping very young children on regular early-bedtime schedules and helping their imaginations grow through reading, storytelling, or play. Older children can share activities with their parents in the evening by playing board games, working on hobbies, and sharing in music or sports.

There have been many questions asked about the effects of cartoons on children. We find in our research that heavy viewing of cartoons leads to inappropriate and disruptive behavior among children in nursery school. Among our elementary school-aged children, the heavy cartoon viewers were rated as "unenthusiastic about school" by their teacher. Even though some parents may enjoy sleeping late on Saturday morning and rely on television as a baby-sitter, we feel they should first become familiar with the shows presented on Saturday mornings and set rules about *what shows and how many* the children can watch.

All children's shows are not alike. Some cartoons involve considerable violence, which agitates children and makes them more likely to tend toward aggressive behavior. Other shows are very frightening in content. The parent should never allow the TV set to substitute for his or her judgment and should establish limits on frequency and content of cartoon viewing. Some parents have claimed that their children are quiet *only* when they watch TV; otherwise they are constantly active or getting into trouble. Thus, the parents particularly like Saturday morning, when the programs are geared to children. Most research, however, suggests that the very active child or the child who gets into fights becomes even more agitated by frequent TV viewing, especially when material involves cartoons, action-detective programs, or noisy game shows. There is no reason to believe that frequent viewing will quiet down a child. Hyperactive children need to learn to play imaginatively and to find resources in *themselves* rather than depending solely on their environment for stimulation. Parents should especially try to restrict such a child's television viewing to shows that they have prescreened and which involve interesting material but little violence. They should encourage such a child to play imaginative games or to work at constructing games out of blocks, Legos, etc.

Active children are also more prone to imitate the acrobatics they see on television. Following broadcasts of Evel Knievel's daring stunts, a surprising number of children in the United States and Canada were injured trying to duplicate such feats on tricycles and bicycles. Even with parental explanation, young children may not grasp all that is involved in developing such skills. Older children are more aware of real dangers and are less inclined toward rash imitation. When such stunt events are broadcast, parents of preschoolers should take a firm stand in the family and simply watch an alternative show or plan another family event to avoid the temptation of viewing by the children.

Sometimes parents ask us if "soaps" are permissible programs for young children to view. Some mothers have stated that they enjoy these programs and watch them regularly as a relief from housework. They enjoy the company of their young children as they watch together, and yet have wondered if the content is harmful. We believe that neither parent nor child should watch television as a main entertainment source, but rather should try to find more active ways of relieving boredom. Parents should recognize how much children learn by imitation. If they can't control their own TV viewing patterns and find more constructive things to do with children, they can't expect to avoid hooking children on TV. The material presented on soap operas is not always appropriate for young children and may simply be confusing or frightening to them. If parents *do* watch with their children, it is important to point out that these are *stories,* and may be exaggerations of problems that people face.

Some programs that elementary school-aged children watch contain violent acts, fairly explicit sex, and sometimes even rape. Parents have asked if they should laugh off these incidents, divert the children's attention from the screen by chatter or by offering food or snacks, or quickly jump up and turn off the set. We feel that a parent should try to explain that sometimes *some* people behave in this fashion. Use explanations that your children can grasp in terms of their age and ability to understand. It is difficult to always shield a child from exposure to some antisocial act that he may see on TV. Let the child know you are available to *talk* about it. It is always better to deal with the facts maturely than to deny the existence of aggression and sex.

One of the major concerns parents express about television is the effect of violent programs on their children. Research over the past decade has demonstrated that television programs that have violent content lead to aggressive behavior in children, especially those who are heavy television viewers and who have little else in the way of a social life. In Chapter 10, we discuss this important issue more fully. We do suggest that parents restrain young children's viewing of violent programming.

Evidence strongly points to a relationship between the viewing of action-detective shows and aggression. We have also found that such noisy, fast-paced programs as game shows, cartoons, and some variety shows can arouse a child to aggression or jumpiness. Some parents are pleased that their children watch game shows because they feature quizzes on information and word matching. We feel that parents should restrict viewing to the less noisy, less screaming shows. Although potentially a child is exposed to lots of information from game shows, the noisy formats, rapid presentation, and emphasis on competition may prevent a child from really grasping and remembering very much. Instead, the child may be viewing the programs passively. Parents should encourage the child to write or rehearse the questions and answers and to share them. Some genuine learning may be possible, but parents cannot count on the TV to substitute for conversation and real family sharing of knowledge and skill. In fact, our research suggests that light television viewers use longer sentences, more adjectives and adverbs, and more varied tenses than heavy viewers.

Parents are often sensitive about programs that deal with special problems such as adoption, alcohol, drugs, and the handicapped child; yet often such programming can be used by parents to discuss these important and delicate issues with their children. Keeping a mature program off the air may impede discussions of significant, basic experiences.

Television can also offer a family an opportunity to discuss stereotypes. Many parents ask what they can do about the ways in which women, blacks, and old people are presented on television. Parents should remember that it is the discussion, not the viewing, that is important. For example, when commercials depict stereotyped pictures of women, parents can discuss these misrepresentations and suggest to their children that they should rely on their own experience for judging situations, rather than on the television. You might want to say, "Remember those ads are just there to try to get you to buy certain products. They just show so many women cleaning or cooking to show off the products. In our house we all pitch in together to get the work done." The presentation of families and family situations on television can also be misleading to children. Many families are obviously not middle class, comfortable, and physically perfect, and parents must point out that the "ideal" families sometimes presented on television are simply not accurate representations of reality. In this respect television can be a springboard for intelligent and valuable discussions about family differences in income and life-style. Banning such viewing may simply give the material more importance than it deserves, and ignoring such influences may reinforce unrealistic hopes among children and also lead to envy or dissatisfaction with parents.

Children may pick up offensive language from TV,

such as "dingbat" or "meatball." If parents watch programs with their children where characters are ma-
ligned or where offensive language is used, they can
show how the audience is laughing at, not with, the
offender. Sometimes parents who are foreign-born
have asked us what to say to their children, who point
out that people on TV usually don't have accents. Parents can recognize the natural differences in speech.
Here again, one can point up the wide range of differences among families in American society, and at the
same time call attention to the limited representations
on TV of the different ethnic groups.

Finally, there is the question of commercials and
their effects. When children beg for a toy because "ev-
erybody has one," it's important for a parent to convey
to children a realistic picture of what a family can afford
and also to point out how a commercial can mislead
them. Adopting a completely negative approach, however, may simply evoke anger or frustration in the
child, for children are captivated by ads, particularly
those that display a premium, usually a plastic toy fea-
tured in an ad for a cereal. As parents know, children
will generally use the toy once before breaking it or
throwing it away, and may not even like the cereal.
Parents should make sound decisions concerning young
children's food choices and not be swayed by those
"extras." Consistency will quickly teach the pre-
schooler what your standards are. This can be done by
explaining each situation firmly but kindly to the child.
Merely attacking credibility of a famous person who is
peddling a product, or putting down a product because
it is expensive, a luxury, or just a waste may only con-

fuse a child. A simple explanation as to why you are not going to buy the product is more constructive than an attack on either the product or the people selling it.

This sampling of the questions we are often asked could be used as a stimulus for family discussions. As you continue to read the book and carry out activities with your child, the information we present will help to clarify any other problems or concerns we may have only touched on here.

FOUR

WHEN YOU WATCH
AND WHAT YOU WATCH

You're ready now to begin our "home minicourse" to help you and your child understand how television works and how it influences your thinking. We designed the activities that follow each chapter so that all you need is your TV set, some paper, and a pencil. We suggest that you become familiar with each chapter before you start to teach your child. It would be best to follow our order of presentation, but feel free to choose any lesson that you think is interesting or important to your family. Depending on your child's age, you may want to put our ideas into your own words, simplify some of the concepts, and choose the appropriate activities. You might want to do one lesson a week, or perhaps two, again depending upon your time and your child's ability, interest, and motivation. Check through the chapters before you begin. The exercises focus on television content, but the information and activities should stimulate learning and language arts skills such as vocabulary building and critical thinking.

HELPING YOUR CHILD TO WATCH TV INTELLIGENTLY

Before we get to the television lessons, you might want
to get a sense of how much television you and your
children actually watch in a typical week. You should
keep a record of the number of shows viewed each day
and how long each member of the family watches
them. Once you have this information, you can make
some decisions about the amount of viewing you do: Is
it too much? Is there one family member watching
more than anyone else? Are you viewing any programs
together? If so, how many? What kinds of programs are
you watching? Is your child viewing television alone?

If your child is watching a great deal of television, you
should impose some reasonable limits. Check out his
other activities. Does he have friends nearby? Does the
family engage in any joint activities? Can you suggest
a hobby or some games he can play as a substitute? If
your child is viewing television alone, have you prescreened the programs? Are they suitable for his age?

You should be aware if your child is *reading* less as
a result of TV viewing. If your child is reading very
little, you should suggest some books that are related to
his favorite TV shows. There are many good books
about sports, science fiction, cowboys, and fantasy that
would motivate your child to read. *The Hardy Boys* and
Nancy Drew series, for example, inspired many children to read, and *Little House on the Prairie* has been
a library best seller since the TV series began.

WHAT YOU NEED TO KNOW

The goal of this chapter is to help children develop an understanding of the different types of programs that are on TV. Parents are usually unaware of the fact that even though a child might be able to describe a show's content and remember the program's name, he may have no idea of the *type* of program it is. Children often don't even realize that different types of programs exist at all!

Researchers Ronald E. Frank and Marshall G. Greenberg have studied what kinds of television programs people watch. Over a four-year period they conducted personal interviews with a nationwide sample of 2,476 people who were thirteen and older to determine their viewing habits and other leisure activities. These researchers have delineated 14 different television audiences, each preferring particular types of programs. For example, the youngest group of male adults, with an average age of twenty-nine, preferred the adventure and drama programs where the hero triumphs, such as science fiction adventure, crime drama, and movies. These men were apt to spend their leisure time fishing, camping, or doing auto repairs. Teen-age male students who were interested in competitive athletics and mechanical activities preferred sports events 105 percent more than the average person in the sample. The people in the sample who watched educational television with their children were mainly women, about thirty-four years of age, white, suburban, whose children's average age was nine. These viewers also preferred television dramas and movies. The most affluent segment, and one of the best educated, were men and women about thirty-six years old, with diverse intellectual and cultural interests. They preferred book-related programs, documentaries, news, and talk shows. People in this group were also the heaviest users of print media: books, magazines, and newspapers.

Children, like adults, have varied preferences for particular kinds of programs. Preschool children generally prefer cartoons, situation comedies, and noncartoon children's programs; first and second graders enjoy situation comedies; and eleven- and twelve-year-olds cite action-adventure shows as favorites (although by these ages children also enjoy watching music, variety, and dramatic programs).

Mariann Winnick, Professor of Education, and Charles Winnick, Professor of Sociology, working in a study with about 300 children aged two to fifteen, found that cartoons represented 43 percent of the programs watched. Situation comedies accounted for 20 percent of this sample's viewing, while educational programs accounted for only 18 percent. The study also showed that boys up to age nine were more likely to watch cartoons than girls, a finding we arrived at in our own research with 340 children. In two of our studies we found that elementary school-aged children rarely watched educational programs on public television, and clearly preferred situation comedies such as *Mork & Mindy* and fantasy-adventure shows such as *The Incredible Hulk.*

There are some sex differences in viewing patterns among children. Boys, for example, tend to watch more violent cartoons, western, crime, and action-adventure shows than girls. As boys grow older, they view more sports and public-affairs programs, while girls watch situation comedies and some variety shows. Young children watch news programs only occasionally until adolescence, when they begin to watch the news on a more regular basis.

Phillip Mohr carried out a study in Kansas and found that among the 5,282 children in fourth through ninth grades in his sample, situation comedies were the most popular. He also found that boys preferred police, science fiction, animal, game, and news programs, while girls preferred musical-variety shows, family dramas, and adult situation-comedies. Mohr found no particular type of show which would be the most popular among both adults and children if broadcast during the family viewing period. Parents, according to his study, exerted very little control over specific programs viewed. They seemed to pay more attention to *when* the children viewed than to *what* they viewed. As for Saturday morning viewing, 92 percent of the 4,882 parents interviewed provided no guidance, and on nonschool nights 75 percent of these parents imposed *no* limitation on the amount of television their children could watch.

Similarly, Temple University's Institute for Survey Research found that in a sample of 2,000 children ranging in ages from seven to eleven, more than 50 percent reported that they were allowed to watch *whenever* they wanted, and more than one third stated they could watch *whatever* they wanted. As a result many of these children were watching adult programming—including action-detective and dramatic shows—with content geared toward more mature audiences.

Research examining why children watch television suggests a variety of reasons. The studies of television in the 1950's indicated that children sought escape through the medium. Eleanor E. Maccoby, in her study of children's television viewing habits, noted three ways a child escapes when watching TV: (1) the child forgets his problems; (2) the child lives through characters who are sexual, aggressive, and disobedient; and (3) the child experiences wish fulfillment, attaining vicarious satisfaction by identifying with the hero. Wilbur Schramm and his co-workers state that a child can be entertained passively and escape from real life boredom by watching television. Cecilia von Feilitzen, in a survey of three- to fifteen-year-olds in Sweden, proposed that there are five main reasons children watch TV: (1) entertainment and emotional fulfillment, (2) information, (3) a substitute source for social contacts with other children, (4) desire to escape, and (5) the special characteristics of the TV medium, such as images, technical effects, and sound. Robert W. Wood and Charles E. Eicher, using a television viewing questionnaire with 745 students from grades 3 through 8, reported that most respondents watched television for the following reasons (and in this order): entertainment; it keeps them company; knowledge and information; and because their parents have turned the set on. Howard Tolley, in a study of almost 3,000 elementary school children, found that television was far more frequently cited as the major source of information about the Vietnamese War than parents, teachers, or any other media. The interpretation of the events, however, was related to parental views.

Let's now review the different kinds of TV programs that are available. There are *adventure programs,* such as *The Six Million Dollar Man, The Incredible Hulk, Emergency!, CHiPs,* and *BJ and the Bear.* Some of these are more realistic than others. The events in *Emergency!,* for example, could happen in real life, while the adventures in *The Six Million Dollar Man* often use fantasy. *Cartoons* such as *Popeye, The Flintstones, Woody Woodpecker,* and *Superfriends* are make-believe and *animated.* To produce an animated effect, a camera photographs many hundreds of different drawings—each representing a different movement. When the drawings are all run together, the characters and objects seem to move.

There are *comedy programs* such as *Mork & Mindy, Happy Days,* and *Laverne & Shirley.* The characters are realistic; they do and say things that people in real life can do, but people like Mork and Fonzie are created by the script writer. We also have drama on television, such as *The Waltons, Family,* and *Little House on the Prairie.* There are funny moments on these shows, but usually the characters are dealing with more serious matters. The Waltons have touched on problems that many families face, such as serious illness, concern with finances, problems with school or friends, birth of babies, and even death. Most of the people on these programs are also realistic, and, like characters in comedy shows, are made up by the writer.

Sometimes television networks present *educational programs* such as *Animals, Animals, Animals* and *The Electric Company* (to help children read and learn numbers); *Jacques Cousteau* (specials about life underwater); *3-2-1 Contact,* (a program to teach children about science); and programs for preschoolers, such as *Mister Rogers' Neighborhood* and *Sesame Street.* There are also *game shows* (such as *Hollywood Squares, Wheel of Fortune,* and *Concentration*) which award contestants prizes or money if they answer various questions correctly.

Serials, or *soap operas,* are dramatic presentations of a continuing story. The plots of these shows are varied, with many interrelated subplots and side stories. Many of the conflicts and mysteries remain unresolved at the end of each show, and a viewer must tune in the next day to find out what happens.

Sports programs deal with practically all sports in the United States. Many of these programs are broadcast in the evening or on weekends when parents—especially fathers—are most likely to be watching. Sports programs have one advantage over almost all other forms of TV programming—they contain "instant replay." That means a segment of the game can be presented over by the camera because the picture was kept on tape or film. You can see a part of the game a second or even a third time. This is especially useful when there is question about a foul in a game, or a winning point. The camera in effect repeats the play for the audience. If this happened in a dramatic show or during a comedy, it would seem strange to us to see the action repeated. That would take away from the effect the writer had in mind—to make his story seem as natural as possible and as close to real life.

Talk shows are very popular on television. On these programs a host or hostess interviews famous people or experts in various fields who offer the viewers some new or unusual information. Often entertainers sing, dance, or enact a part from a current play or movie, and writers introduce and talk about their new books. Occasionally people such as drug addicts, single parents, adopted children, or handicapped persons will discuss and share their lives with the viewing public. Once in a while a person with an unusual experience appears on a talk show and describes it to the audience. This may be someone who has survived a disaster, seen a UFO, or made some important discovery in the sciences.

Variety shows are primarily for entertainment. *The Osmond Family, Carol Burnett and Friends,* and *Saturday Night Live* are shows featuring comedians, singers, dancers, and musicians. We can see ridiculous scenes on these shows, or sometimes a clever comic will satirize serious issues and institutions, such as politics, religion, and the government. Variety shows usually have a host or hostess who appears each time.

Finally, we have the *news programs.* Television news can instantly bring us in touch with every part of the world and create a personal feel in a news story. These programs are usually made up of three segments—international news, national news, and human interest stories. The newsperson usually presents the most important news story first and saves the lighter human-interest stories (the rescue of a child from a burning building, an elderly person's special birthday, a reunion of a family after many years, etc.) for later.

It is a difficult task for a news team to select the events for an evening news program. One half hour of the evening news may entail a full day of preparation, including the gathering of the news, writing, rewriting, editing, filming various segments, and making decisions about the order of presentation, the placement of commercials, and how long each segment of news should run.

TV news writers have the difficult job of presenting all the news and still leaving room for nightly features such as sports, weather, food tips, and movie and play reviews. Sometimes networks can present a subject in greater depth by using a *documentary* format, a news program which reports at length on special subjects, such as farmers, nuclear energy, forests, or endangered animals. Reporters can use interview techniques, library film, actual pictures of the event or of the subject, and a variety of camera techniques to keep the audience interested.

In addition to news programs and documentaries, we have the *television news magazine,* such as *Prime Time, 60 Minutes, Thirty Minutes,* and *Hot Hero Sandwich.* We get some news, some in-depth coverage of a special topic, and some features involving interesting personalities. Sometimes there are in-depth interviews conducted with one or several people, such as *Meet the Press.* The people interviewed here usually offer their opinions about important events concerning politics, the economy, and international affairs. We also see *special coverage* news programs when an entire show is devoted to detailing some current news story, such as a disaster (like a flood or an earthquake), a visit from a dignitary (like the Pope), or a program highlighting the elections or a political debate.

Newspeople often try to present news stories that

can be accompanied by interesting pictures. A news
item about a flood, for example, is always more dramatic than an item about the cost of living, even though
the latter information affects a greater number of people. Choices must be made constantly about how to
present the news, but most newspeople try to be fair
and they aim to be truthful.

SPECIAL WORDS AND IDEAS FOR CHILDREN TO REVIEW

Adventure programs—*The Six Million Dollar Man, The Incredible Hulk*

Cartoons—*Popeye, The Flintstones, Woody Woodpecker,
Superfriends*

Comedy programs—*Mork & Mindy, Happy Days, Laverne
& Shirley*

Dramas—*The Waltons, Family, Little House on the Prairie*

Documentaries—*60 Minutes* and *Prime Time* include brief
documentaries

Educational programs—*3-2-1 Contact, The Electric Company, Jacques Cousteau*

Game shows—*Hollywood Squares, Wheel of Fortune*

News programs—*CBS Evening News, The MacNeil-Lehrer
Report, NBC News*

Serials—*All My Children, As the World Turns, Another
World*

Sports programs—*NFL Football, World Series, Wide World
of Sports*

Talk shows—*Merv Griffin, Phil Donahue, Dinah!*

Variety shows—*The Osmond Family, Carol Burnett and
Friends*

DISCUSSION IDEAS

Use the list of types of programs as your starting point. Talk about sample programs for each type. Try to get your children to point out the special characteristics of each category, and why a particular program falls into it.

Find out if your children prefer one type of program format compared to another. Ask them why.

Watch a type of program that your children rarely watch. See, for example, if you can interest them in documentaries or educational programs.

Discover which kinds of programs the family generally prefers to view together. Have the children list these and talk about why these particular programs appeal to the family. What are the elements in the program?

Older children need to be encouraged to read newspapers if they want a more detailed account of an event. By the time children are in junior high school, they may be cynical about television. It is therefore important for them to understand that TV content is controlled to some extent. Children in the middle grades (5 to 8) are old enough to learn how TV news can at times appear to distort an event by presenting only part of the story. For example, you and your children may want to discuss how a political speech may be shown on TV. The director may choose to show the part of the speech where an audience cheered enthusiastically, or where they heckled the speaker. Very often, there will not be time to show both parts. In a case like this the complete story is not being presented, and a viewer may be left with an inaccurate impression of what actually took place. Even if the newscaster describes the "other side," most viewers will remember what they *saw* more vividly than what they *heard.*

ACTIVITY 1

Explain the program categories to your child. When you watch television with your child, see if he can tell you the correct categories for the programs. Here is a sample of an activity you can do together.

TV Program Categories

Name one or two programs that belong under the categories listed.

Cartoon   *Comedy*

_____   _____

Drama   *Game show*

_____   _____

Movie   *News*

_____   _____

Sports   *Talk show*

_____   _____

Variety show

_____

Serial (soap opera): a continuing story

_____

Documentary: a program about a real event

_____

Kindergarten and first grade children may just name the type of program rather than write it. They may only be able to describe a few of the programs, such as sports, cartoons, comedies, or game shows. Try not to expect too much from your child, and don't frustrate your child by demanding that he learn more than he is ready to learn.

ACTIVITY 2

Ask older children (grades 5 to 8) to write down a typical day's viewing by listing how many of each type of program they watched. For example, on Monday a child might watch one news program, one variety program, and three comedy shows. If your child wants to, he can keep a record for a week, and fill in each category.

ACTIVITY 3

DIFFERENT TYPES OF TV PROGRAMS

BE A TV DETECTIVE. TRY TO FIND *PICTURES* OF EACH TYPE OF TV PROGRAM. LOOK IN THE NEWSPAPER OR IN *TV GUIDE* FOR PICTURES THAT MATCH THE SHOWS BELOW.

Comedy	Family Drama	Adventure	Variety	News	Sports	Game	Cartoons	Children's Shows with No Commercials.

ACTIVITY 4

1. Watch the news with your child. Write down the order of presentation. On another night, turn to a different channel. Watch the news. Was the order the same—did international news come first, for example?
2. Compare a news story in your evening newspaper with a story on TV. What items are omitted?
3. Are different kinds of products advertised during network news than on local news? Why?

SUGGESTED READINGS:

Prime Time School Television has a unit on the news which is available free of charge. Prime Time School Television, 120 South LaSalle St., Chicago, Ill. 60603.

Using the Newspaper in the Classroom As a Resource for All Subjects., Beverly T. Schultz, The New Haven Register and Journal-Courier, 367 Orange St., New Haven, Conn. 06503.

FIVE

HOW TELEVISION WORKS

For many children, TV characters may seem like real people who somehow appear on the screen. To a small child, even news programs and game shows seem magical. The first step in "de-mystifying" television for your child is to teach the basics of how television programs are made and broadcast.

Research has shown that many young children believe that TV characters actually live in the TV set or travel from the set, through the plug, and into the wall. Although most elementary school children have a more sophisticated understanding of TV, they may not really understand that actors only pretend to be characters, and that writers and directors create the programs that the actors star in. Although it is not necessary for your child to understand all the details of television production or electronics, children of all ages can understand and appreciate some basic information. When children understand how television works, they can think about what they like or dislike about the program and how they would like to change or improve it. This understanding is therefore a prerequisite for the critical thinking that we'll be talking about in the following chapters. The information and vocabulary words are also relevant to other topics that your child will learn in school.

Sometimes news shows, awards programs, or TV specials will show the camera operators at work, or directors and engineers watching the TV monitors in the control room. If you are on the lookout for these kinds of examples, you can use such programs to help you illustrate the information presented in this lesson.

GOALS

The two major goals of this lesson for your child are:

- To develop an understanding of what TV is—how it becomes the picture on the TV set at home and in school
- To develop an understanding that many different people are needed to put together a TV show

WHAT YOU NEED TO KNOW

Has your child ever asked you how television works? Many parents find it difficult to explain how that electrical box in their house can show scenes from many different parts of the world. The word *television* comes from two words, *tele*, a Greek word meaning "far away," and *videre*, a Latin word meaning "to see." Your child may be interested to learn that *television* means "to see far away" and may be curious about how television does this.

HOW TV COMES TO YOUR HOUSE

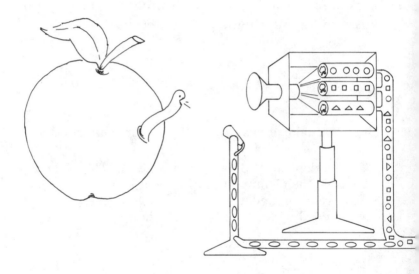

A television camera has a *lens* that can be pointed at whatever will appear on the screen. The lens focuses the light from the scene onto the camera tube. The camera changes the picture into an electrical signal. A television set can change that signal back into a picture. It's not quite that simple, but that basic explanation is enough for most children. If you look closely at a TV picture, you can see that it is made up of little dots. Show your child that a black-and-white TV has black and white dots, and that a color TV has colored dots.

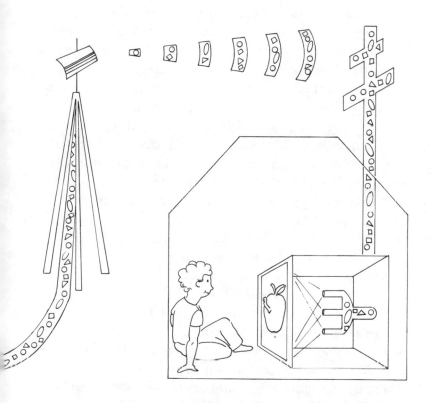

Some of the dots glow very bright, and some are dim-
mer. These dots make the bright and dark areas of the
picture on the TV screen. A TV camera doesn't "see"
a picture the way our eyes do. Instead, it sees a picture
as dots on a line, one dot at a time, one line at a time.
There are hundreds of dots on each line and 525 lines
in each TV picture. Therefore, the camera works very
quickly, making a new picture 30 times each second.
Because the camera is so fast, our eyes don't see the
pictures change. Instead, we see all the pictures run-

ning together as a moving picture. When these dots and lines are changed into an electrical signal, this signal is sent over a wire to a television set, or *broadcast* into the air so that the televisions can pick up the signal on their *antennae* and change it back into pictures. The sound for the TV picture travels through the air at the same time, so we can enjoy picture and sound together.

When children understand that many people help to make a TV program, they can better understand the medium. It's a good idea to start with the person with the program idea: the *producer.* A program might start with the producer's own idea or someone else's, but the producer is in charge of getting together the people and materials needed to make the program. The *script writer* writes down the ideas in the form of the necessary dialogue and directions. When the script is finished, it will include most of the directions for how the program will look and sound. The *director* handles all the remaining decisions that have to be made. He directs each of the people who work to make the program; he picks the actors and decides how they will act and speak their lines from the script; and he helps them during rehearsals. Your child need not remember all of this information, but he or she should understand that the programs are based on a script that actors memorize, and not on the spontaneous activities of real people and situations.

Your child probably does not realize that houses and other locales depicted on TV are often not real. You can explain that the *set designer* draws pictures of the places (called *sets*) where the actors are supposed to be. Your child may have difficulty understanding that a set can be a kitchen, castle, front yard, or any other kind of place. Of course, programs sometimes use real surroundings, but often carpenters and painters make the sets. A person in charge of *props* takes care of the furniture, plants, and other objects that help to make the set look like a real place.

Many parents are less knowledgeable about other personnel involved in TV programs. During rehearsal the *camera operator,* acting on the director's instructions, manipulates the movement of the camera to film a scene in the clearest or most interesting way. The *lighting director* makes sure there's enough light for the television picture and also uses the lights to simulate any time of day or night.

When the rehearsals are finished, preparations are made to do the scene just as viewers would see it at home. The director and engineers, sitting in the control room, work with the machines that make the sound and picture for the program. From this vantage point, the director can see what each camera operator sees, through small TV sets, or *monitors.* The director instructs the camera operators over the telephone *headset.* While the engineers are getting their equipment ready, the cast members are busy putting on their costumes and makeup. (All actors have to wear makeup; without it, the bright studio light would make them look pale.)

Show your child the names of people who do this kind of work, before and after a favorite program. Explain that the lists of names are called *credits,* because they give credit to the people who helped.

SPECIAL WORDS AND IDEAS FOR CHILDREN TO REVIEW

Actor—a man or woman who plays a certain character in a TV program

Airwaves—carry electrical signals from the TV studio to your TV set at home

Antenna—The air is full of TV signals sent from many stations. These signals are caught by an antenna.

Audio—the sound part of a program

Broadcast—to send pictures and sound by television

Camera operator—the person who works the TV cameras. The camera operator takes orders from the director.

Credits—the list of names of the people who make a TV program

Director—the person in charge of making the TV program. The director decides which props to use, how the actors should act, and which camera to use at a certain time.

Engineer—the person who is in charge of the electrical equipment at a TV station, such as the TV lights, video and audio equipment, and TV cameras

Microphone—also called mike. Microphones pick up the voices and sounds that are part of a television program. The sound is changed, like the picture, into electrical signals.

Network—a group of TV stations connected by electrical signals all over the country so that they can all receive the same TV programs and commercials. The three commercial networks are ABC, CBS, and NBC. Since TV programs cost a lot of money to make, local TV stations can't make many programs. The networks make TV programs that are shown all over the United States, so they are able to sell broadcast time to sponsors at a higher rate than local TV stations.

Picture—what you see on your TV

Producer—the person who creates and organizes TV programs. The producer is in charge of finding and spending the money it takes to make a TV program. He or she makes other important decisions, such as which script or actors to use.

Rehearse—to practice using the words and actions used in the program

Scene—TV programs are divided into different parts. Each part is called a scene.

Script—the written text of both the picture and sound parts of a TV program

Script writer—the person who writes the story to be used in a TV program

Sound—what you hear on your TV

Studio—a special room for making television productions. Each studio is soundproof. Most studios have at least two TV cameras and special kinds of lights.

Television set—a receiver that picks up electrical signals in the air and turns them into the picture and sound on your TV screen

TV camera—A picture begins in the TV camera. There is no film in it. Its job is to change the picture it sees into an electrical signal that can be sent through wires and across space. Three or four large studio cameras are used to take pictures on an average TV program.

TV screen—the front of the TV set where you see the picture

TV station—where the TV studios, cameras, and other TV equipment are located. The electrical signals that are carried through the airwaves to your TV set at home come from the TV station.

Video—the picture part of the program

Videotape—The sound and picture electrical signals are recorded on videotape so that a TV program can be edited and broadcast at a later time. Videotape can be played back immediately.

DISCUSSION IDEAS

Show your child a photograph from a newspaper. Let your child use a magnifying glass to discover the black and white dots of which it is composed. A comic strip can be examined to see how color dots are used. The following questions may be helpful.

1. What colors are the dots?
2. What colors do you see when you look at the picture from farther away?
3. Why do you see shades of gray in a picture made up of black and white dots?
4. Why do you see colors that aren't really there?

Help your child see that the TV picture is also made up of dots or grids.

Using the diagram of the transmission process, go over the process with your child.

Briefly explain the different jobs involved in making a TV program. After you have explained this information, watch a program with your child and see if he or she can point out the following:

a set
a prop
an actor or actress.

Try to give an example of what the lighting director or camera operator contributes to the program.

ACTIVITIES

1. Make a list of the writers, producers, or directors of several favorite programs. This information is shown on the credits before or after the program, but the credits are sometimes on the screen so briefly that your child may need your help in listing the names.
2. While watching a black-and-white TV, imagine the colors of the characters' eyes, hair, clothes, house, etc., and write these down. If you have only a color TV, tune the color out.
3. Imagine that you are a script writer. Write a four- to-eight sentence new ending for a TV program that you watched this week.
4. Imagine that you are a producer. Write down your idea for a new TV program.
5. Imagine that you are a set designer. Draw a picture of a set for a TV program classroom scene. Write down the props that you will need.
6. *Family Activity:* Your family might want to pretend to prepare a short scene for a TV program about a family. Family members can take on the jobs of the producer, script writer, director, set designer, propman or propwoman, makeup artist, camera operator, lighting director, and actors.

SUGGESTED READINGS

There are many children's books which explain how television works and describe the many jobs involved. They include illustrations that are especially helpful. The following list of children's books is provided to give you an idea of some of the books that are available:

Bendick, Jeanne *Television Works Like This.*

Corbett, Scott *What Makes TV Work.* A scientific approach to TV.

Lerner Publications *Television As a Profession.* Pictures and vocabulary.

MacDonald Educational *Television.* A picture book that explains how television works.

MacDonald Educational *The Movies.* A picture book explaining movies and cartoons.

Polk, Lee, and LeShan, Eda *The Incredible Television Machine.*

Unstead, R. J. *See Inside a Television Studio.* Photographs may be helpful: text is appropriate for ages eleven to twelve.

SIX

TV MAGIC: EFFECTS
AND SPECIAL EFFECTS

When the *The Six Million Dollar Man* bends a steel girder with his bionic hand, when *Wonder Woman* leaps from a tall building and lands unharmed on the ground, or when David Banner is transformed into *The Incredible Hulk,* a kind of "magic" is taking place before our eyes. Adults recognize that the camera and special-effects team is at work, but children may need help in understanding how reality is distorted on television. Many different effects and special effects are used to make television programs appear more interesting and exciting. These techniques sometimes help children to understand a program's plot, but they can also be distracting and confusing, especially for younger children who have trouble distinguishing between reality and fantasy.

The purpose of this chapter is to help children learn more about the effects and special effects used on television, including camera shots, slow motion, sound effects, different kinds of props, and editing. If children can understand how and why these techniques are used, they can learn more from the programs they watch.

GOALS

The three major goals are as follows:

- To teach parents and children to recognize the types of camera effects used on most TV programs: zoom, close-up, long shot, pan, dissolve, wipe
- To demonstrate how special effects are used to distort reality
- To develop vocabulary pertaining to effects and special effects

WHAT YOU NEED TO KNOW

All television programs use effects and special effects. Close-up shots on news programs, for example, focus one's attention on what the newscaster is saying. Or when a photograph accompanies a story, the camera backs away from the newscaster for a long shot so one can look at the photograph *and* the newscaster.

Action programs, programs with superheroes or science fiction characters, and many other shows that are popular with children use a greater assortment of special effects, which children can learn to recognize. Although these techniques affect children greatly, they have been studied more often by advertisers than educators. Advertisers have learned, for example, that children will keep their eyes on commercials that use exciting special effects and that quickly change from one camera shot to another. *Sesame Street, The Electric Company, Hot Hero Sandwich,* and other television programs have imitated the quick pace of commercials to keep young children watching the set. However, these techniques are not necessarily useful in helping children *understand* what they are watching.

Research conducted by Gavriel Salomon at Hebrew University in Israel and by John Wright and Aletha Huston-Stein and their colleagues at the University of Kansas has shown that certain camera effects help children understand programs. For example, when the camera zooms in for a close-up shot of an object in a room, and then zooms out again for a view of the whole room, a child can better understand exactly where the object is. This is important if the viewer is supposed to notice that the object is missing later in the program. However, if zoom shots or other effects are used to emphasize unimportant parts of a story, they will often distract and confuse young children. As a result young viewers may forget the more important elements of the story. If, for example, a child watches an action program with many exciting violent scenes, he or she may forget the line of the plot or fail to realize that the "bad guys" are punished in the end. Researcher Mary Field and her associates in England found that children between the ages of seven and eleven had difficulty with long shots, unexpected loud sounds, blaring music, and abrupt cutting from one scene to another.

We are also concerned about the impact special effects may have on children's imagination and creativity. When a child reads a fairy tale, he or she must imagine the scene and think about what is happening. But when a child watches the same fairy tale on TV, all the fantasy and creativity is in the hands of the producer, director, actors, camera operators, and program editors. The child can passively watch the program without ever thinking about the story. However, if your child understands how effects and special effects are used, any program can become a "puzzle" to think about and solve.

Changing reality through the use of a camera is known as a *camera effect.* The simplest way to do this is to move the camera. If, for example, the camera is moved from side to side, the viewer will see different parts of the room as if he were turning his head. This technique, *panning,* can show that different people in the televised room see it from different views, or panning can be used simply to take the viewer from one character to another. This kind of movement makes a program more interesting than if the camera merely showed the viewer the whole room for the entire scene.

It is also possible to change the way the camera sees just by changing its height. Placing the camera down low can make an actor look bigger, and placing the camera up high can make an actor look smaller.

Changing the Height of the Camera

Here is a picture of Ralph taken with a TV camera.

When the TV camera is held near the ground and is
TILTED UP, this is how Ralph will look.

When the TV camera is held up high and is TILTED
DOWN, this is how Ralph will look.

Many television cameras have a zoom lens that can
zoom into the picture for a close-up view, then zoom
out again. The lens can zoom very quickly or so slowly
that you hardly notice it. You can probably find an
example of these basic camera shots on any television
program.

The Zoom

THE ZOOM LENS: ZOOMING IN AND ZOOMING OUT

Here is a picture of Tommy taken by a TV camera.

This TV camera has a special lens called a ZOOM lens.
Without moving the TV camera, you can very quickly
make things look closer or farther away by turning the
ZOOM lens. When you turn the ZOOM lens very quickly
to make things look closer, you are ZOOMING IN. This is
how Tommy would look if the TV camera ZOOMED IN.

When you turn the ZOOM lens on the TV camera very
quickly to make things look farther away from you, you
are ZOOMING OUT. This is how Tommy would look if
the TV camera ZOOMED OUT.

When the director of the *The Six Million Dollar Man* program wants to show how a bionic eye works, he uses the camera effect called a *zoom,* which creates the illusion that the bionic man can see things very far away. There are other effects as well, including lighting and sound effects such as rain, lightning, and thunder. One can create a lightning effect simply by moving a piece of cardboard in front of a studio light. Sounds of rain and thunder can be recorded and then played back whenever they are needed.

All the effects in television that take us from one picture to another require the use of a *switcher.* The director can use this device to *cut* quickly from one shot to another; he can *dissolve* slowly to the next picture; and he can have one scene slowly *fade* away as the next scene fades in. The switcher also enables the director to *wipe* from one shot to the next. A wipe, as illustrated below, can move in many different directions and assume a variety of shapes.

Wipes

Top row: horizontal wipe, vertical wipe, corner wipe, diagonal wipe; bottom row: circle wipe, four-corner wipe, horizontal-split wipe, horizontal sawtooth wipe.

The Split Screen

You can create a split screen effect by stopping a wipe in the middle of the screen. Each half of the screen will present a different picture. To set up for a split screen one camera must put one object in the left half of the viewfinder, the other in the right half. The unnecessary part of each picture is then wiped out.

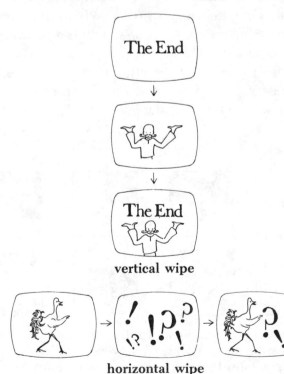

vertical wipe

horizontal wipe

The switcher also lets the director superimpose words and pictures on a main picture. The *Today* show, for example, opens with the name of the show "supered" on a picture, then dissolves to the hosts in the studio. The picture cuts to close-ups of the hosts as they tell about that morning's program, and then cuts to a wide picture that lets you see the newscaster. On another network, *Good Morning America* uses wipes to put together pictures of the different people who appear on the program, then dissolves to the hosts in the studio. Watch these programs with your child and take turns naming the camera effects, using our illustrations for references.

The switcher can also create the "chroma-key" effect. In the illustration on the next page, an actress is standing in front of a blue wall. If the director wants the actress to be standing in a different environment, he can set up slides or a moving picture of any locale in the background. The actress in the studio cannot see this background, but to the television viewers at home (as well as the TV monitor in the control room), it will look as though the person is actually standing in front of the scene. In the picture it seems as if the actress is standing in an actual forest; in fact she is *still* standing in front of the blue wall. This technique is called *chroma-key* and is used often on television. News programs, for example, always use chroma-key to show photographs behind newscasters. Sports programs also use this technique frequently. When sportscasters introduce a football game with an entire stadium in the background, they are really sitting in

front of a blue wall in the studio with a shot of the
stadium chroma-keyed behind them.

Chroma Key

(left) Color slide of trees provides background for the key
effect.

(center) Studio camera takes a picture of a woman
standing in front of an evenly lighted blue background.

(right) The completed chroma key effect transports the
woman into the landscape.

When directors want people to disappear on TV, or
when they want other impossible events to occur, they
can choose from a variety of special effects. Programs
such as *I Dream of Jeannie* and *Bewitched,* for example,
often show people vanishing instantly. Creating this
illusion is a relatively simple matter. In the photograph
at right, the magician waves the magic wand and holds
very still while the little boy simply walks away. The
director won't want the TV audience to see the boy
leaving, so he simply *edits* that part out. The finished
scene will look as if the boy suddenly disappeared.

Editing: Making Someone Disappear

Editing can create other special effects as well. When
you watch a superhero jumping higher than humanly
possible, you may notice that the jump doesn't happen
in one picture. Instead, there are three views of the
actor jumping. In the first view the actor has started to
jump. In the second view he seems to be moving
quickly through the air. That is really a second jump,
which may have been from a trampoline. The third
view shows the actor landing at the top. This is actually
the end part of a third jump. The three taped jumps are
then edited together to look like one long jump. Parts
which show the trampoline, the end of the first jump,
or the beginning of the third jump are edited out. Scenery can also be changed to make the jump seem even
higher.

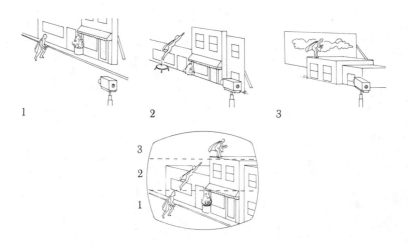

Editing: A Bionic Jump

Another kind of special effect is *slow motion,* a technique often used on superhero programs to emphasize the action (notice how many fighting sequences are shown in slow motion). *Fast motion* is sometimes used on these same programs to make the hero's running seem superfast. Both effects are achieved simply by speeding up or slowing down the tape or camera.

There are many other kinds of special effects, and often several of them are used together. For example, if a program shows two people being chased in a car, the actors are probably not in a real automobile, but in a machine that has car seats, a steering wheel, and no tires. The machine can't be driven, but it shakes as if it were swerving around corners. The camera tapes close-up shots of the actors' faces so the viewer does not see most of the machine. Meanwhile, a chroma-key of a videotape of streets and other cars is used as a background for the scene. Sound effects of screeching tires and honking horns are also used. The tape of the people talking is then edited together with the tape of a real car chase.

SPECIAL WORDS AND IDEAS FOR CHILDREN TO REVIEW

Chroma-key—This is a way of combining two entirely different pictures so that they appear to be one solid picture. The actor can be put right into a scene, not just in front of it. It is used to make actors look much larger or smaller than their surroundings; to make it look as if they are moving quickly from one place to another; or to make people who are actually in different places appear to be together.

Close-up—a camera shot which makes the object or person seem very close to you

Cut—a quick change from one camera to another, without an overlap of the pictures

Dissolve—a slow change from one camera shot to another, so that you see both shots for a short time

Edit—to electronically "cut out" unwanted parts of a video-tape recording of a TV program and save the pieces that are wanted. The result looks like a single continuous program.

Freeze-frame—holding a single, nonmoving picture on the screen

Pan—turning the camera from side to side, so that you see what you would see if you were turning your head

Shot—each picture that the camera takes

Slow-motion—The normal speed of the camera is slowed down, making the action look slower than it is.

Split screen—The screen is divided into two or more parts and each camera shows its picture on one part of the screen.

Wipe—an electrical effect that makes one picture seem to push another picture off the TV screen. Wipes can be made in many shapes, including circles growing larger or a line moving across the screen.

Zoom—Without moving the TV camera, objects or people can be made to look closer or farther away by using a zoom lens attached to the camera. *Zoom-in* means turning the zoom lens to make an object look closer than it really is. *Zoom-out* means turning the zoom lens to make an object look farther away than it really is.

DISCUSSION IDEAS

Can TV superheroes really do all those impossible things? If they can't, how is it that we see them do these things on TV? Special effects can make us think we're seeing something that isn't really happening. It's a bit like magic.

Go over the words and effects with your child. Find some programs that use these effects. Ask your child to name them as you view the program together. Keep a list of the effects you find. See how many you can discover in just one evening.

ACTIVITIES

1. Pick one of the following special effects. How do you do it?
   a. A bionic eye sees a man a long distance away—the eye is large on the TV screen
   b. A person turns into a monster
   c. A witch makes a girl disappear
2. Which programs use slow motion? Why do they use slow motion? What would the scene look like without slow motion?
3. Write a story about a superhero. At the end of the story, list the kinds of special effects you might use if you made a TV program about your story.
4. Make three drawings to show how a "bionic" jump is made for a TV program.
5. Which TV programs show people disappearing? Make a list.

SUGGESTED READINGS

The following book would be helpful for this lesson:

MacDonald Educational *The Movies.* A picture book explaining movies and cartoons.

SEVEN

REAL AND PRETEND ON TV

In a discussion about creativity in writing fiction and in scientific research Albert Einstein once said, "When I examine myself and my methods of thought, I come to the conclusion that the gift of fantasy has meant more to me than my talent for absorbing positive knowledge." (*The New York Times Magazine,* February 18, 1979).

Imagination is a basic human characteristic, probably with us at birth, but which develops according to an individual's upbringing and education. Our imaginative capacities can help us reconstruct old memories and form new thoughts, and they can provide us with a medium for future planning, self-entertainment and aesthetic appreciation or creativity. In this chapter, then, we examine the very critical impact that television and make-believe play may have on a child's imagination.

There is reason to believe that daydreaming originates in the fantasy play of childhood. Evidence indicates, for example, that children fantasize as early as eighteen months to two years of age, and by three years of age one can observe a considerable amount of make-believe play. In a whole series of studies we have seen a variety of constructive possibilities for such pretend play in early child development.

We list here some of the specific benefits for children between the ages of three and six who are able to engage in games of fantasy. We know of such advantages of early make-believe games because we can observe the differences between children who show such patterns early and those who don't. The fact is that by ages three or four some children are already regularly engaging in pretend play whenever they can.

Self-entertainment and Positive Emotionality

We find considerable evidence that kindergarten and preschool children involved in make-believe play show positive emotions and smile and laugh often. Children who have this capacity to create an imaginary world appear happier than those who do not engage in games of fantasy.

Delaying Capacity, Waiting Behavior, and Development of Defenses

Freud pointed out that one function of the ego is to defer gratification and to delay rash, impulsive behavior. Our evidence clearly indicates that children who have the capacity for fantasizing are better able to tolerate periods of delay, resist temptation, and develop stronger defenses against the expression of anger and distress.

Vocabulary and Cognitive Skills

Children often talk out loud when they engage in make-believe games. By doing so, they can hear their own words and try out new combinations of words and phrases. Our data show that children who play games of fantasy also have command of a more complex vocabulary and grammar.

Empathy

Research indicates that children who engage in make-believe games take different roles as part of these games. Sometimes they are the heroes, sometimes the "bad guys." They have periods of victory and moments of failure. As a result of such role-playing, children learn to empathize with the plight and emotions of others.

Role-Rehearsal

The very nature of make-believe play requires children to act out many of the roles they must adopt later in their lives. In kindergarten, children learn how to deal with these roles through the use of symbolic and imaginary games. Children actually rehearse games such as school, going to the doctor, taking a trip, etc. In effect they are preparing themselves for a wide variety of situations they will have to confront as they grow up. Naturally, in a more extended way this role-rehearsal forms a part of the adult's fantasy capacities—a person willing to play out many possible situations will be better prepared for those situations when they actually occur. There is even evidence which indicates that gymnasts, skiers, basketball players and other athletes who engage in mental as well as physical exercise do better than those who do not rely on their imagery and fantasy capacities as part of the training procedure.

Planning and Foresight

An important potential outgrowth of the skills in imagery and fantasy a child develops may be the capacity for planning. We know that extremely impulsive adults and adolescents show very little evidence of imagination and fantasy on psychological tests. Early practice in pretend play may therefore be important in helping the child develop a mental set in which different possibilities and plans can be tried out before one embarks on a hasty course of action.

Aesthetic Appreciation and Creativity

Finally, evidence suggests that the imaginative capacity, particularly in later childhood, adolescence, and adult life, is related to the ability to appreciate the art forms. We have learned to play out some of our previous experiences on a mental screen. We also can relive scenes from movies or books or ballets, and we can enjoy in memory the fine moments of a symphonic concert or great sequences of play in an athletic event. The human imagination therefore has an important role not only in the development of our basic capacity to learn and organize new information but in the more general enrichment of our day-to-day life.

We must quickly add one point about imagination for those who are inclined to think that imagery and fantasy processes reflect immature, neurotic, and psychotic forms of thought. Research evidence suggests that many individuals who are emotionally disturbed have failed to develop control over their imaginative resources. Often their fantasies are repetitive and extremely limited in scope. In many cases individuals who have had emotional difficulties or who were engaged in antisocial behavior have not learned to use their own imagery and fantasy capacities well. There is also evidence from research with children and from observations with adults, that individuals who have developed their imaginative capacities are better able to differentiate between their own thoughts and hallucinations; that is, they have learned a more precise distinction between reality and fantasy by having practiced and identified fantasy experiences over the years.

FACTORS IN EARLY CHILDHOOD CONDUCIVE TO IMAGINATIVE DEVELOPMENT

We are only beginning to explore what early childhood experiences cause children to engage more regularly in make-believe games. We shall briefly summarize here some of the major results from research, literature, and clinical observation.

One could argue that the child, in order to develop the imaginative capacity more fully, needs what might be called novel material or interesting information to assimilate. Jean Piaget, in his analysis of early childhood development, argued that a child tries to repeat and integrate new material with his previously established ideas. In the course of such attempted assimilation, we see playful behavior and much of what we often regard as "cute." A child of four was observed by his mother lining up all of his toy soldiers on the kitchen floor. When asked what he was doing, he replied, "I'm getting them ready to rescue Daddy. You were talking on the telephone and said he couldn't come home for dinner because he was tied up at work!"

There is reason to believe that children who have little opportunity to communicate with adults (or who don't have a chance to overhear more complex vocabulary) may participate less in make-believe play. There is also evidence that children from lower socioeconomic backgrounds use a very limited vocabulary. Studies in many crowded inner-city or culturally disadvantaged homes suggest that parents often talk very little to their children except for giving quick commands like "Be quiet," "leave your sister alone," "time to eat." When children from such backgrounds are given a chance to play make-believe games, their vocabulary becomes more diversified and new words and grammatical constructions are practiced. In homes where parents have the time or inclination to tell children stories, to talk about the family history or about their own childhoods, we find that children develop more elaborate and interesting plots in their make-believe play. If given the opportunity to engage in such play, children can expand their use of language.

Evidence also suggests that the amount of privacy a child has for practicing make-believe games may be important. Similarly, there are indications that toys that are not clearly symbolizing a person, but are somewhat more neutral, such as blocks, Legos, or clay, will lend themselves to a greater variety of play situations.

Probably the most important factor in the development of children's imaginative capacities is their relationship with parents, uncles and aunts, older siblings, etc. Goethe wrote:

From Father I have looks and build
And the serious conduct of living.
My Mother gave me gaiety
And zest for fantasizing.

(Xenien)

We know from an increasing body of research that adults who take the time to play with, tell stories to, and read to children play a crucial role in the development of their imagination. Research has also shown that adults who get children involved in a game or a story and then gradually step away to allow the child's own interest and motivation to take over, are most likely to encourage spontaneous make-believe play.

We have tried to make a strong case for encouraging imagination in children and ultimately in adults. We believe the imagination is of great importance not only for the emotional pleasures it can bring but also because it is tremendously useful in handling information, in planning, and in creative activities.

Those of us who listened to radio shows before televi-

sion became so widespread were able to conjure up
mental pictures of Buck Rogers, Flash Gordon, Jack
Armstrong, and The Shadow. If we were to describe
the characters or settings, we all would have different
versions of their features, clothing, habits, etc. We
played a more active role listening to radio than we do
while watching TV. We know from our own research
experiences that many nursery school children imitate
sequences from programs viewed in the past. One vivid
scene we noted was a child pretending she was Wendy.
She sat in a makeshift house "cooking," while her friend
pretended she was flying, spreading her arms like
wings, running around the room shouting "I'm Peter
Pan." Two others were acting out the pirate scene re-
plete with make-believe alligators and a cruel Captain
Hook. One could speculate that the highly imaginative
child needs to withdraw from the set periodically to
actively play out the material he sees. The constant
stimulus of television programming may actually be
interfering with the child's own "game plans." Other
children watch television with intense concentration
and thus do not withdraw from the set to play out material. We need to compare these two viewing styles to
see whether or not the highly imaginative child views
television with the same degree of intensity as the less
imaginative child. Perhaps intensive viewing has no
effect on a child's ability to *extract from television,* and
imagination is more critical than the degree of concentration. We have found, for example, that during a
viewing of the *Mister Rogers'* show most of the children
in our study did *not* stay glued to the television screen.
Yet when compared to children who were riveted to a

showing of *Sesame Street,* the children viewing *Mister Rogers' Neighborhood* did as well in tests pertaining to material remembered from the show as did those watching *Sesame Street.* It may be that *Mister Rogers'* repetition of various words and phrases enabled the children to process the material even though the set did not hold their undivided attention.

We are interested in whether or not television can lead to imitation of events which are later brought into a child's make-believe game. Although little research has focused on television's impact on the imaginative potential of children, studies are dealing with the positive effects of television. But the question of extending behaviors such as cooperation, sharing, and helping (what psychologists call prosocial behaviors) to instances other than direct imitation of acts portrayed on the television programs has yet to be demonstrated. F. Leon Paulson, for example, stated that children showed cooperative behavior paralleling those acts shown on *Sesame Street,* but did not carry these acts over to other situations in their daily lives.

In one of our studies, we compared the effects of two kinds of children's programs on the imagination of preschoolers. We found that children who were rated low in imagination at the beginning of the experiment and were exposed to ten sessions of the *Mister Rogers'* program over a two-week period made significant gains in imagination when compared to children who viewed *Sesame Street* for that same period. The *Mister Rogers'* program, with its clear-cut distinction between reality and a make-believe kingdom, appears to stimulate imagination, as well as socially useful behaviors, in children. Friedrich and Stein also found gains in three- to five-year-old children's imagination after exposure to the *Mister Rogers'* program. The experimental condition involving prosocial television, related play materials, and teacher training and involvement produced the most consistent effects on both positive social interaction with peers and imaginative play.

In our long-term follow-up project we are studying imagination and its relationship to television. We observed 340 children to collect data on their imagination, aggression, concentration, cooperation, peer interaction, and mood states. We interviewed the children about television viewing habits and TV-related games and toys they own, and we also questioned them about imaginary playmates, favorite games, whether or not they had "pictures in their head," and if they had daydreams. The parents had been keeping detailed records of what programs the children viewed during two-week probes every three months. Parents were also interviewed about their children's viewing habits, and whether their children have imaginary playmates. Data thus far seem to suggest that children who are light television viewers report significantly more imaginary playmates than those who are heavy television viewers. It is interesting to note that girls are more likely to use both female and male TV characters as imaginary playmates (Superman, Bionic Woman), while boys only identified with male superheroes. The children who had imaginary playmates also exhibited more adaptive play and more developed language, in addition to watching less television than the other subjects.

Robert P. Snow asked 50 preadolescent children what their favorite programs were, and if they thought the shows were "real" or "make-believe." All of the children could identify cartoons as make-believe and news as real (although there was a split of opinion about shows like *The Brady Bunch*), and they were able to recognize a difference between their own make-believe play and real situations. The children also stated a preference for make-believe television which they could relate to their own play. Interestingly, these children did not describe *Road Runner*, a cartoon, as violent, because they classified it as make-believe. Thus, when the child can distinguish between real and make-believe, the impact of violent action in fantasy shows is lessened, according to Snow. Furthermore, in this study the children were also able to make distinctions between "funny" and "serious" violence in television.

In contrast to Snow's subjects, who were all in the ten-to-twelve age range, Ralph J. Garry did a study with preschool and primary-grade children. Garry found that these younger children accepted what they saw on television as real. Westerns were less disturbing to them than crime and detective stories, which were closer to real life. A great deal depends on how similar a situation on TV is to one that a child observes in his or her own life. According to Garry, events on television which portray other children have a greater impact on young viewers, especially if they are of the same age and sex.

Cartoons do seem to affect children's creativity, as measured by scores on Guilford's creativity tests. Stanley L. Stern divided 250 mentally gifted fourth, fifth, and sixth graders into seven groups—six of which were to watch specific categories of television exclusively. The control group had no instructions. After three weeks of viewing, subjects were tested on an alternate form of Guilford's test of creativity. Results indicated that children who watched cartoons had the greatest decrease in creativity scores. Stern views this trend as important in terms of the long-range effects of indiscriminate viewing by children. Surprisingly, he found that watching educational television also decreased creativity scores. The study, though ambitious, has some methodological flaws and needs to be repeated by other researchers.

Grant Noble has carried out numerous studies examining effects of television on children. He found that children played less constructively after viewing realistic aggression, and more constructively after seeing very artifical or ritualized aggression—e.g., knights jousting or cowboy shoot-outs. Noble also suggested that five-year-olds have more difficulty in determining what is real than do six-, seven-, and eight-year-olds. He found that in retelling stories they had seen, the five-year-olds added people and objects that were not in the film. They were also unable to comprehend when a story ended. They embellished stories with their own imaginative people and ideas.

Elihu Katz and David Foulkes reported that middle-class children experiencing difficult parent-child relations, and children isolated from their peers were heavier television viewers, with the latter group specifically preferring adventure stories. This use of fantasy-oriented media appeared to be related to disparities between a child's aspirations and those of his peers or parents. The authors wondered whether such programming drained off discontent and enabled children to understand themselves better, or if it led a child to withdraw from the real world and to confuse real situations with fantasy.

In some of our own research, children in grades 3, 4, and 5 who watched fantasy-violent programs were less cooperative, less successful in their interpersonal relationships, less happy and less imaginative. We also found that children who spent more time reading watched fewer fantasy-violent programs. They may have been able to satisfy their interest in adventure through reading and imagination, and relied less on television as a source of excitement.

In a study of 30 children exposed to either *This Is Your Life* or *Sports Day,* Grant Noble reported that 14 thought that the people on the set had spoken directly to them, and 6 of the children answered back. The reality of the set for these children involved them in "conversation" with the television characters. In our work with preschoolers we have heard them respond to Mister Rogers when he asked questions. Actually, Fred Rogers allows this response by use of "still" moments, when he does not talk, but expects a child to interact with him. This gives a child the opportunity to repeat the message and store it.

Modeling behavior is important and, as mentioned, has powerful effects on children. One area that remains relatively untapped is the use of television in day-care centers as a model to teach children how to play and

become more imaginative. If teachers had materials
related to specific television formats, they could serve
as mediators and reinforce particular messages, ideas,
or concepts through related activities. In one of our
studies, for example, when Mister Rogers presented a
puppet show about "Jack and the Beanstalk," a nursery
school teacher then very successfully used materials
and puppets to get the children to use their imaginations.

Our experience leads us to believe that if children
learn how to play, and use their imaginations actively,
they can make a clearer distinction between reality and
fantasy. The child who says "let's pretend" has had the
practice of moving between the real world and the one
of his imagination. If television presents material confusing to the young child, parents can help clarify these
confusions by watching programs with their children
and explaining how certain effects introduce the world
of fantasy on television.

GOALS

- To recognize whether parts of a program are real or imagi-
  nary and to distinguish between the different elements of
  reality and fantasy
- To learn about the process of animation
- To learn the difference between animation and live action
- To recognize the importance of music and sound effects in
  TV programs
- To develop familiarity with vocabulary relevant to the
  topic of fantasy and reality

WHAT YOU NEED TO KNOW

Television employs many techniques to create illusions and a sense of fantasy. People seem to talk to each other freely, without pausing or hemming and hawing the way we do in real-life conversations. They snap clever remarks and "put downs" back and forth at each other with a speed we can never attain when we're conversing with people. This illusion of rapid speech, of quickness of wit, is produced by careful rehearsals, and by editing out of a tape the natural pace of speech. Thus, even many of the "live" events on TV are prerecorded on tape and carefully edited. Sometimes the "voice-over" comments of sportscasters, which show great perception about a particular play or athletic maneuver, are actually recorded *after* the events by simply having the speaker's remarks recorded as he watches a video playback. To the viewer it looks as if the sportscaster knows more than he does.

Editing and "smoothing out" a tape of real people on talk shows or news programs is one way of creating an *illusion* of reality. Another way of creating a sense of reality can be seen in "docudramas," films based on real events but with actors portraying the actual persons whose lives are depicted. TV dramas such as *Eleanor and Franklin* or *Brian's Song* (a program depicting the lives of the football players Brian Piccolo and Gale Sayers) all use professional actors to play persons who once lived.

TV also presents actors who portray characters that seem very real although actually they are fictional productions of the screen writers. Fonzie on *Happy Days,*

for example, seems to many people as real as someone
they know from school or work, and Mary Tyler Moore,
the actress, played Mary Richards so convincingly on
The Mary Tyler Moore Show that many people confused the actress and the fictional character.

There are also programs like *The Six Million Dollar
Man* or *The Incredible Hulk* which depict actors doing
things that we know are *impossible.* Cartoons portray
characters performing impossible deeds as well, although children understand that the people they see in
these programs are not real.

It may be easy for children to understand that drawings are not real, but it is not so easy for them to understand when actors create illusions. Children may
believe, for example, that actors are hitting each other
in fights when in fact they are missing one another
entirely. By using a variety of techniques, such as furniture which breaks easily, sound effects, and menacing
music, a TV director can very effectively create the
illusion that characters in fights are being hurt.

Many other methods can be employed to distort reality: make-up can be used to help characters look
strange; the camera can make people look small like
the Lilliputians on *Gulliver's Travels,* or enormous like
The Hulk; costumes can add to the fantasy or make-
believe element in programs; and lighting effects can
create the illusion of bright sunshine or darkness.

SPECIAL WORDS AND IDEAS FOR CHILDREN TO REVIEW

Cartoons or *animation*—Separate drawings are photographed one at a time on film or videotape. When they are all shown together, it looks like the cartoon characters are moving.

Costumes—clothes and jewelry worn by the actors to make them look like the characters that they pretend to be

Fiction—a pretend or made-up story

Live—a TV program that is broadcast at the same time it is really happening

Makeup—powder, lipstick, eyeshadow, and other cosmetics used on the skin to change an actor's appearance

Nonfiction—a story about something that has really happened

Props—furniture and other objects used by actors to make the set look like a real place

Stunts—difficult, dangerous, or unusual actions such as jumping through a window, falling out of a tall building, or driving a car at high speeds through city traffic

Taped—a TV program that is recorded on videotape so that mistakes can be taken out. The program is broadcast at a later time.

DISCUSSION IDEAS

1. If your child watches fantasy programs like *The Incredible Hulk* or *The Six Million Dollar Man,* ask your child: "Is The Hulk a real person? Do the people on that program really exist? How do you know? How can you tell when something on TV is real?"
2. Have your children name some programs that depict real people talking about real events; programs that have actors portraying real events; and programs with actors por-

traying realistic fictional events: "How can you tell the difference? What are actors? What is the difference between an actor and a character? Include information about how makeup, costumes, and props make people or events seem different than they really are (e.g., *Eleanor and Franklin*)."

3. Discussion of programs where animated characters portray realistic events: "In what ways are the Flintstones realistic?" (e.g., They do things most people do.) "In what ways are they pretend?" (e.g., Cave dwellers did not have dinosaurs for pets, did not drive cars, etc.)

4. Discussion of programs where animated characters portray impossible events: "In what ways are the Superfriends (animated Batman, Wonder Woman, etc.) realistic? In what ways are they pretend? What other animated characters do impossible things?"

5. Ask your child: "How are cartoon animals realistic? In what ways are most cartoon animals unrealistic? (Why are they portrayed as wearing clothes and living like humans?) Name some animals that seem to survive impossible danger." (e.g., Road Runner and Wile E. Coyote fall off cliffs, but are never hurt for more than a few seconds.)

6. Have your child name some programs where actors engage in impossible actions. (Examples include *Mork & Mindy, Wonder Woman, The Six Million Dollar Man, The Incredible Hulk, I Dream of Jeannie, Bewitched*.) "How can you tell that these are not realistic?"

ACTIVITIES

1. Set up a chart like the one below. Your child can draw pictures or cut and paste pictures of a fantasy character, a real person, and a realistic character in the space provided. Then he or she can list the real people and television characters in the correct columns.

2. Have your child list the programs that he watched this week that had real people talking about real events; then the programs that had animated characters. Which type of program did he watch more often?

Reality and Fantasy on TV

Look at the names listed at the bottom of this page. Have you seen any of these people on TV? Some of them are *fantasy characters,* some are *realistic characters,* and the rest are *real people.* Write the names of the characters or people that you have seen in the correct rows.

Draw a TV Fantasy Character Here:	Draw a Real Person on TV Here:	Draw a Realistic TV Character Here:

Fantasy Characters	Real People	Realistic Characters
_____	_____	_____
_____	_____	_____
_____	_____	_____
_____	_____	_____

Mork

Richie Cunningham

Donald Duck

Henry Winkler

Popeye

Marie Osmond

Mary Tyler Moore

Roger *(What's Happening)*

Mindy

David Banner *(The Incredible Hulk)*

Carol Burnett

Joe Hardy *(The Hardy Boys)*

3. Write a story or poem about an imaginary person.
4. Write a story about the things you did today. Would that make an interesting TV program? Now change the story to make it more exciting or humorous.
5. List some characters that are portrayed by actors and as animated characters. Would you rather see cartoon characters, or would you rather watch a program where the same characters are portrayed by actors?
6. Draw a cartoon character.
7. Look in a TV guide to see if there are any documentaries or docudramas on TV this week. List them.
8. Which programs use music to create a feeling of mystery or suspense? List them. Watch carefully this week and write down the programs that use music. Turn off the music during an exciting part. How did you like it without music?
9. Make up a tune to go along with a television scene.
10. If you watch a program that shows a fighting scene, write

down the sound effects, props, or makeup which made the scene seem real.

11. Draw a person. Draw the same person on another sheet of paper, then change his or her appearance as if you were using makeup (do not erase).

12. If you have watched a TV program about real people (Examples: *Backstairs at the White House, Eleanor and Franklin, Brian's Song*), read a book about the same person. How was the TV story different from the book?

SUGGESTED READINGS

Children may want to read books that deal with real events that have also been depicted on TV programs. Your local library probably has children's books on the following:

Pearl Harbor   Helen Keller
Amelia Earhart   Brian Piccolo
Eleanor Roosevelt   Franklin Roosevelt

EIGHT

CHARACTERS WE LOVE AND HATE: LEARNING ABOUT OURSELVES THROUGH PEOPLE WE MEET ON TV

Parents are a child's first model for developing a sense of identity. The young child regards his parents as powerful, perfect, beautiful. He is also aware of the seeming injustices a parent may bestow on him when he is punished or prevented from doing something he desires. This process of identification and search for self begins in early childhood, continues through adolescence, and, as some psychologists believe, goes on throughout one's life. Erik Erikson, a prominent psychologist, suggests that most children go through two stages of identification: one when they are about four to six years old, and another during adolescence. Identifying with parents of the same sex and learning the appropriate behavior for males and females in society is a task of childhood. During adolescence, young people must not only reaffirm their sexual identities, but begin to form mature sexual relationships and think about questions relating to ideologies, ethics, and occupational choices.

With the advent of the women's movement, and the increasing changes in society concerning women's role, it is interesting to note that television still perpetuates, to a large degree, the stereotyped sex-role models and lags behind the current trend toward expanded role models, especially for women.

As we will see in our lesson on stereotypes, television depicts males in a wider range of occupations than females. More males are in dramatic network programs, and in general both males and females are shown in stereotypic roles. We may therefore wonder whether or not these characters exert any influence over children's identification patterns.

As children get older and enter school, teachers become increasingly important in their lives, and even parents of other children offer them new models for identification. Television, movies, books, and magazines suggest different occupational models for children, and certainly the heroes and heroines in any story offer a young person physical and psychological models beyond the immediate family. In order to finally achieve a sense of self, a child must be aware of his own physical makeup, his strong points as well as his inadequacies; and he must develop a feeling of consistency in life-style which would include his own particular way of growing, thinking, dressing, acting, and achieving.

How, then, does television play a role in helping a child develop a sense of identity? Remember how many women imitated Farrah Fawcett-Majors's hairdo after seeing her as a female detective on *Charlie's Angels*. Ask yourself if you have ever bought a product because you believed it would help you look like a television superstar. TV characters and celebrities influence our choice of clothes, the way we talk, our hobbies and interests, the way we decorate our homes, and even the way we behave. Children are especially likely to imitate the clothes, hair styles, and behaviors of the TV characters that they admire. This may include using new expressions such as "Shazbot" from *Mork & Mindy,* or pretending to be a favorite superhero.

Children usually find it easy to talk with each other about which television characters they like and dislike. However, they may have more difficulty expressing *why* they feel the way they do. This lesson provides parents with an excellent opportunity to learn more about their children's feelings, to help their children understand their own feelings, and for parents and children to discuss their values together.

GOALS

There are four major goals for this lesson.

- To understand how TV influences our feelings about and knowledge of ourselves and our relationships
- To develop an understanding of one's own positive and negative feelings about TV characters by thinking about subtle traits in addition to the superficial traits
- To compare the positive and negative traits of TV characters with those of characters from literature, films, and the people we know
- To develop vocabulary pertaining to identification

WHAT YOU NEED TO KNOW

You should first remind your child (as we've mentioned earlier) that most actors pretend to be different characters on television. You can use the example of Robin Williams, who plays Mork on *Mork & Mindy*. Your child may also have seen Robin Williams on *Laugh-In* or in the movie *Popeye*. Remind him that producers, directors, writers, and actors create these characters.

The next step is to help your child think about why people like certain TV characters. You may want to point out that we often like characters who are somewhat like us or who enjoy what we enjoy. Popular TV characters are often funny (like Mork or Lucy) or strong and successful (like The Six Million Dollar Man).

Have you ever thought about why your child likes superheroes? Because children are relatively small and weak, with very little control over their environment, they enjoy watching characters who are powerful. They can vicariously enjoy the control that these characters have over other people. (Of course, adults often like these characters for the same reasons.) In one of our studies we found that the most consistent play theme over a year's time by both boys and girls involved characters from television—generally superheroes such as the Bionic Man, Batman, and Wonder Woman. We also found that both boys and girls had imaginary playmates based on television characters, again superheroes.

One interesting result we noted in our research is that girls could identify with both male and female characters, but the boys seemed to prefer only the males. Children also enjoy and identify with television personalities who are warm, funny, silly, and daring. These characters can exert a considerable influence over a child. For example, when Evel Knievel made his daring jumps on television, many children (especially boys) ended up in accidents using makeshift ramps and their bicycles. Other characters, such as Laverne, Shirley, Mork, and Fonzie, can also affect the behavior of a child.

Parents should also understand how children learn and respond to role models. According to researchers Craig Edelbrock and Alan Sugawara, female preschoolers have clearer expectations for adult feminine behavior than males have for male adult behavior. The researchers found that boys were more likely to prefer programs portraying males in play (not adult) activities. The researchers explain that children are first exposed in life to female adults (mothers, day-care workers, preschool teachers) and thus girls have clearer feminine adult role models to emulate. Boys, on the other hand, must eventually shift away from female to male role models. Because fathers may not be around as much, peers may serve as stronger models than adult male figures. Boys may also turn to TV, where indeed there are more men than women portrayed in exciting and interesting roles.

In addition to serving as role models, characters on detective programs and even on situation comedies may provide children with an outlet for their anger and frustrations. For example, children may identify with characters who express anger openly. They can do this by copying their style of walking, talking, and even their aggressive behaviors. If the characters are pre-

sented as powerful and competent, and receive re-
wards for their behavior, children may indeed try to
emulate them.

You may want to help your child compare the negative and positive traits of television characters. Many
young children (grades kindergarten through 4) do not
understand what "personality traits" are. They may
find it easier to talk about what characters do rather
than what kind of people they are. The traits that they
can talk about are relatively superficial: strength, at-
tractiveness, popularity, and humor. Parents may want
to encourage children in this age group to think of
other traits as well, such as happiness, kindness, and
helpfulness. For example, many children (especially
boys) say that they admire The Hulk because he is
strong, but they may be oblivious to the character's
tormented and unhappy life. However, if children are
asked specifically whether The Hulk seems unhappy,
many children are able to talk about this aspect of
his character. With help from you, your children can
learn to understand that when David Banner is out of
control he becomes The Hulk, and that it is this loss
of control which leads to his distress and torment.

Children in the middle grades (5 through 8) may also
focus on a character's superficial traits at first, but they
can easily be encouraged to make more sophisticated
judgments. Parents may want to encourage these older
children to talk about more subtle, positive traits such
as altruism, affection, industriousness, and loyalty; and
negative traits such as greed, vengefulness, and shal-
lowness.

Work by psychologists Aletha Stein and Lynette

Friedrich as well as our own research has indicated that positive role models on programs such as *Mister Rogers' Neighborhood* (for young children), *Black Beauty,* and *Swiss Family Robinson* can improve cooperation, sharing, and turn-taking. Roderic Gorney, David Loye, and Gary Steele in California found a significant decrease in aggressive mood in adult males after just one week's exposure to special programs which emphasize positive traits (such as *The Waltons*).

Encourage your child to think about the way characters behave in different situations. Children often like the predictability of characters: They enjoy knowing how Fonzie or Mork or Laverne will act in any given situation. For this reason, children may enjoy watching a weekly program because they feel they know the characters personally.

As a parent you should be aware of your child's favorite characters. Have you ever heard your child discuss TV characters with friends? Friends' opinions often influence children's attitudes. And, of course, the script writers, directors, and actors also manipulate the audience's feelings about TV characters. For example, viewers know how they should feel about Fonzie because they see how much other characters on *Happy Days* admire him. Children like Mork because he is funny and can do many strange things, but Mork is also a very kind and loyal person who tries to make people happy. And when children see *Starsky and Hutch* and similar detective characters on TV, this tells them that these characters are admirable even though they sometimes kill people. You should make sure that your child understands that this kind of character is not admirable *because* he kills people. With these and many other TV characters, children should understand that characters can be both good and bad.

By talking about television characters, children can learn about other people and themselves. Parents can help children understand why they like characters and how these feelings influence their own needs and goals.

SPECIAL WORDS AND IDEAS FOR CHILDREN TO REVIEW

Character—any kind of person that a script writer or actor makes up

Expressions—the showing of different feelings by moving the face and body in different ways

Identification—when you think that another person has qualities or traits like your own

Identity—the different qualities or traits that a person has that makes that person what he or she is

Idol—a TV or movie character that you like a great deal

DISCUSSION IDEAS

Ask your child who his or her favorite TV character is, and why. Children may want to make a list of TV characters and put stars next to the characters that they like. Next, they can underline the characters that have some traits that are similar to their own. The following questions may be helpful: "In what ways are they like you? In what ways are they different from you? Is it fun to watch TV characters that seem similar to you? Do you think any of these characters could be called 'good' or 'bad'? Is it possible for a character to be both 'good' and 'bad'?"

Parents should make sure that their children name traits other than superficial characteristics such as strength, beauty, popularity, or humor. An example of a discussion of a character follows: "What is The Hulk like? What is good about being strong like The Hulk? What is bad about being strong like The Hulk? Is David Banner, or The Hulk, a happy person? How do you know?"

Discussions can precede or follow the viewing of a favorite program.

ACTIVITIES

1. Name something that Mork (or another character) would never do.
2. Complete analogies or compose analogies on the activity page.
3. Name someone from a book, or a friend or neighbor, who is like a favorite character. How are they alike?
4. We sometimes like characters who seem ideal, because they can do things that we can't do. Name one, and list the traits that describe him or her.
5. Change a TV character to be more likable.
6. Make up a character that you'd like to see on TV or to be with.
7. Draw a favorite TV character.
8. Compare characters in a book with the *same* characters on TV (see Suggested Reading).
9. Family Games:
   a. *Choosing Favorites.* Each family member says which

character he or she would like to be and why. Family members discuss what they like or don't like about those characters.

b. *Who Am I?* Each family member lists four traits or mannerisms of a TV character. Other family members try to guess who the character is.

Example: Archie Bunker could be described as prejudiced, possessive about his favorite chair, demanding, beer-loving, or using the "Bronx cheer."

c. *Opposite Traits.* One family member names a trait of a favorite TV character. Other family members try to name a character with the opposite trait.

Example: Laverne is silly.

Serious characters include: Mrs. Walton, Charlie's Angels, Lou Grant, Mr. Ingalls, Billie Neuman.

SUGGESTED READINGS

Parents may want to suggest books with characters that are similar to the children's favorite (or least favorite) TV characters.

The following books have been adapted for television, and the children may be interested in comparing the book characters with the TV characters. These books are usually available in school or local libraries.

Barrie, J. M. *Peter Pan*
Clymer, Eleanor *Luke Was There*
Dixon, Franklin W. *The Hardy Boys* series
Gates, Doris *Little Vic*
Mazer, Harry *Snow Bound*
Wilder, Laura Ingalls *Little House on the Prairie* series

These books are sixth grade or junior high level:

Baum, Frank L. *The Wizard of Oz*
Crane, Stephen *The Red Badge of Courage*
Haley, Alex *Roots*
Kerr, M. E. *Dinky Hocker Shoots Smack*
Taylor, Mildred *Roll of Thunder, Hear My Cry* (a Newbery Award winner)

ACTIVITY PAGE

Characters We Love and Hate

Analogies show the way that different things are related to each other. Complete these analogies.

1. Popeye is to Olive Oyl as Mickey Mouse is to ____ .
2. Ma Walton is to Pa Walton as Edith Bunker is to __ .
3. Fonzie is to *Happy Days* as Barbarino is to _____ .
4. The Hulk is to David Banner as Superman is to __ .
5. Richie Cunningham is to _____as Roger is to Dee.
6. Laverne is to *Laverne & Shirley* as Lucy Ricardo is to _____ .

Now try these:

1. Mork is to *Mork & Mindy* as _____is to *I Dream of Jeannie.*
2. Mrs. Ingalls is to Laura Ingalls as _____is to ____ .

NINE

TV IS ONLY PART
OF THE PICTURE

Television is an unrealistic world inhabited by young, healthy, middle-class white people. While it is true that blacks, the elderly, foreigners, and handicapped people appear on television more than ever before, they are often cast in stereotypic and negative roles. Women in particular are depicted unrealistically. These misrepresentations create problems because most children assume that TV programs depict life as it is or the way it should be. All too often, then, it is possible for children to form their opinions about minority groups on the basis of television's inaccurate portrayals.

The purpose of this lesson is to teach children about stereotypes. We examine the many stereotypes of families, police work, men's and women's roles, racial and ethnic groups, the elderly, and handicapped people in an attempt to teach children that we are all members of different groups which are neither good nor bad, but are an integral part of our collective environment and reality.

GOALS

The three major goals of the lesson are as follows:

- To introduce the idea that even "realistic" programs do not necessarily present an objective view
- To understand that it is not appropriate for TV viewers to generalize about groups from the examples seen on TV (e.g., minority groups, women, elderly, handicapped)
- To develop an understanding of the concepts of "stereotypes" and "prejudice" and related vocabulary words

WHAT YOU NEED TO KNOW

Television can be a wonderful teacher. It can show children what life is like for other people around the world and throughout history. However, many children do not realize that most TV programs are made to entertain rather than to teach us, and they may not understand that a program can be realistic in some ways and very unrealistic in others.

Most children display a greater understanding of family programs, such as *The Brady Bunch* and *Eight Is Enough*, than other shows. They may assume that these programs portray family life as it *should* be, but they realize—based on their own firsthand experiences —that real families have greater difficulties solving their various problems.

On the other hand, children may be less critical of programs that depict unfamiliar people and places. For example, police officers on TV are usually involved in suspenseful, dangerous activities. Many children, not realizing that real police officers rarely fight (and in fact spend a good deal of their time directing traffic or typing reports), develop a stereotypic picture of policemen continually chasing and shooting people.

Most of the television research in the area of stereotypes has concentrated on race and sex roles. Research during the 1960's and 1970's, for example, indicates that there were relatively few nonwhite and female characters on television. Only one-third of all TV characters were women, and most were in the smallest, least important parts. Nonwhites made up only 10 percent of all television characters, and they were also in the least significant parts. Both women and nonwhites tended to be portrayed in traditional, stereotypic roles, and were often depicted as dependent on or subordinate to white men. There were also very few TV characters (particularly females and blacks) under the age of sixteen or over the age of forty.

Nonwhite characters are more likely to be victims or criminals than white characters. Although there are now several programs with black characters, shows very often perpetuate harmful stereotypes of black people as fun-loving, lazy, and unsuccessful. Very few are depicted as serious, intelligent, or hard-working, partly because almost all blacks on television are in comedy programs.

Research studies have shown that television has far more power to influence children's attitudes than may have been previously believed. For example, when children watch programs that portray black people favorably, their attitudes toward blacks become more positive, whereas programs that portray black people negatively will increase children's negative attitudes toward them. In another study 40 percent of the white elementary school children surveyed stated that they learned about black people from television. In an instance such as this, it is impossible to ignore the impact of television on children's beliefs and attitudes.

In our research we found a clear relationship between the programs that children watch and the prejudicial attitudes that they express. For example, white children who watch more programs with major black characters (such as *Good Times* or *Diff'rent Strokes*) are less prejudiced against black people. These characters, while often silly and stereotypic, are warm, caring people and present a relatively positive image, especially for white children who know few black people. In contrast to these findings, children who watch more violent television programs (which often portray blacks as villains or victims) tend to be more prejudiced against black people. Although these programs may not *cause* prejudice, they may encourage and reinforce it. Unfortunately, a child often does not understand that these shows aim to be entertaining rather than educational. In fact, children may misunderstand the intent of realistic, higher quality programs: In one class that we studied, a child who had watched *Roots* asked why the black people did not want to drink at the white people's water fountain! It is discouraging that a program which was intended to teach people about racial prejudice could be so badly misunderstood by a child. This provides a good example of why it is important for parents to watch TV programs with their children and encourage them to ask questions.

The research on female TV characters has shown that there have been improvements in recent years. Women on TV are no longer limited exclusively to lower-status tasks and silly or incompetent behavior. However, new stereotypes are developing. The new, more liberated female television character is usually young and beautiful as well as competent. She is almost never married, and spends much of her time falling in love, even though this usually conflicts with her exciting job. If you compare female and male TV characters, you will find that the females are usually much younger, more attractive, and more likely to use their beauty than their brains. Charlie's Angels are good examples. The writers use every excuse to dress these women in bathing suits and seductive evening gowns. The actresses are so beautiful and well dressed that it is almost impossible to believe the plots, which show them fighting crime. Although they are portrayed as competent and successful, their childlike devotion to Charlie —a man whom they never see but seem to idolize— keeps them in their place. They are never portrayed as independent adults in control of their lives. The stereotypes presented here may not seem terribly negative, but it is discouraging to us that our research shows elementary school girls admiring Charlie's Angels more than any other TV characters. When we asked them why, the most popular response was that they are pretty, which suggests that the program encourages girls to believe that beauty is the most important trait for women, even though the show also tries to convey the message that beautiful women can be competent as well.

A recent study by Shirley L. O'Bryant and Charles R. Corder-Bolz that used commercials produced for research purposes found that 60-second commercials can influence children's sex-role attitudes. In this study, the commercials portrayed women talking about how they liked "ZING fruit drink" as well as their jobs. Some of the commercials showed a woman in such nontraditional roles as a butcher, pharmacist, welder, or laborer; the other commercials showed a woman as a telephone operator, fashion model, file clerk, or manicurist. The findings showed that the commercials influenced the children's career preferences, as well as their attitudes concerning appropriate careers for men and women. If a 60-second commercial has this influence, it seems likely that weekly programs are even more powerful in "teaching" children about appropriate sex roles.

In our research we also found a relationship between television viewing and sex prejudice. Girls who watched more game shows and programs that depict women as extremely silly or incompetent (such as *I Love Lucy* and *I Dream of Jeannie*) were more prejudiced against females than were their classmates. Again, these programs do not necessarily *cause* prejudice, but they may influence the girls' attitudes. Whereas adults may watch these shows and think they are funny, children may assume that the programs show how women *should* behave. Parents need to explain to their children that characters like Lucy are not intended to be role models of appropriate behavior.

It has taken television producers a long time to include more positive female characters and minority group characters on television, and even today, television presents only part of the picture. TV portrays working women, but they are rarely mothers or older women. Retired people are rarely portrayed as main characters or as people living full and interesting lives. Since children have distorted perceptions of age, television's failure to portray elderly people functioning normally as grandparents, neighbors, friends, or co-workers encourages children to assume that older people are unimportant and very different from the rest of the population. In addition, the portrayal of handicapped people as unhappy and disturbed individuals whose lives revolve around their problems tends to reinforce any fears a child has about people who are "different." Black people and ethnic minorities seldom are depicted as ordinary people: Race or ethnicity is usually the underlying topic of the program. And, of course, there are many reruns and old movies on TV that present very stereotypic characters. Parents can modify television's potentially negative impact on children by talking to them about television's stereotypes and omissions.

SPECIAL WORDS AND IDEAS FOR CHILDREN TO REVIEW

American Indian or *Native American*—These are two names for the people who lived in America before the settlers came from Europe. Many Native Americans still live in America.

Prejudice—to judge people before you know them, or to already have ideas about them

Stereotyped—the preconceived ideas we have when we think about a person

DISCUSSION IDEAS

1. TV does not always give us an accurate picture of what life is like. Ask your child to think of a program about a family that is different from your family. It may be helpful to discuss this just before or after watching a program like *The Brady Bunch, The Waltons, Little House on the Prairie,* or *Eight Is Enough.*
2. Discuss the fact that most of the important TV characters are usually boys or men, and these males are usually young adults, white, and healthy. TV used to have almost no women stars or black stars, but this is changing. Can your child name some women TV stars? Black stars? White male stars? Compare the number in each category.
3. Not all people are like the ones we see on TV. Children know that not all classes are like Kotter's sweathogs. Ask your child: "Are all white children like the Brady Bunch? How do we know?" Talk about the similarities and differences. Ask: "Are all black teen-agers like the stars of *What's Happening* or *Good Times?* How do we know? Are all women as silly as Lucy *(I Love Lucy)* or Laverne? How do we know?" Explain the word *stereotype.*
4. Pretend that you and your child are visitors from outer space, and you only know about the United States from watching TV. What would you know about each of these?

   working mothers
   handicapped people who live normal lives
   accents (regional: southern, midwestern, New York, Boston; foreign)
   police officers

American Indians or Native Americans
poor people
grandparents or other elderly people
Oriental people
5. Talk with your child about what we know about the fictional planet Ork from watching *Mork & Mindy*. Are all Orkans like Mork? How do we know?

ACTIVITIES

1. Be a stereotype detective. Find a stereotypic character on commercials or TV programs. What are the exaggerated characteristics that make him or her seem like a stereotype instead of a real person?

   a black teen-ager who acts ridiculous
   a helpless or childish woman
   an ugly "bad guy"
   a "dumb blonde"
   a domineering mother
   a "he-man" (who is very strong and never cries or fails)
   a helpless old man or woman
   a pathetic handicapped person
   a "goody-goody" cute boy or girl
   a smart person with glasses

   Clues: clothes, accent, facial expressions, gestures, behavior

   (Or)

   These are types of characters who aren't on TV (in commercials or programs) very often. Can you find any examples of these?

   a working mother
   a serious black man
   a handicapped person who lives a normal life
   a studious teen-ager

an active, working grandmother or grandfather
a man doing housework
2. How can we recognize a stereotypic character?
   Clues: clothes (including aprons, glasses, etc.), the way
   they talk (accents, expressions, special words), behaviors and activities, gestures and physical expressions.
   Find examples on the TV programs that you watch.
3. Read a book about someone who is not like the TV characters in his or her group, or a book about people you
   don't see on TV very often. Some examples are in the
   Suggested Readings section of this lesson.
4. Draw a person in a nonstereotypic role. For example, a
   man ironing, a woman doctor, a black newspaper reporter.
5. Be a reporter: Interview five- to six-year-old children in
   your neighborhood.
   What do boys want to be when they grow up?
   What do girls want to be when they grow up?
6. Activity page: Match the different groups with the examples shown.

SUGGESTED READINGS

These books are available in many school and public
libraries.

Ethnic Groups: Fiction

Gates, Doris *Little Vic.* A black boy trains a racing horse.
The issue of prejudice is raised.
Greene, Bette *Philip Hall Likes Me. I Reckon Maybe.* A
story of a southern black girl. (Newbery Award)
Lexau, Joan *Striped Ice Cream.* An eight-year-old black
girl and her family.

Taylor, Mildred *Roll of Thunder, Hear My Cry.* A story of black children in the South. (Newbery Award; sixth-grade level)

McCabe, Inger *A Week in Henry's World: El Barrio.* Photographs and text of el barrio.

Thomas, Marlo *Free to Be . . . You and Me.* A collection of short stories, poems, and songs.

Ethnic Groups: Nonfiction

Brahs, Stuart *An Album of Puerto Ricans in the U.S.*

Latham, Frank *The Rise and Fall of "Jim Crow."* The black struggle for equality in America.

Lester, Julius *To Be a Slave*

Butwin, Frances *The Jews in America*

Kurtis, Arlene *The Jews Helped Build America*

Wytrwal, Joseph *The Poles in America*

Dowdell, Dorothy and Joseph *The Japanese Helped Build America*
The Chinese Helped Build America

Stanek, Muriel *How Immigrants Contributed to Our Culture*

Reit, Seymour *Child of the Navajos.* A contemporary story of a nine-year-old Navajo boy.

Wiesenthal, Eleanor and Ted *Let's Find Out About Eskimos*

Male and Female Roles: Fiction

Taves, Isabella *Not Bad For a Girl.* The story of a girl who wants to join a Little League team.

Thomas, Marlo *Free to Be . . . You and Me.* A collection of short stories, poems, and songs.

Male and Female Roles: Nonfiction

May, Julian *Amelia Earhart: Pioneer of Aviation*
Warren, Ruth *Pictorial History of Women in America*
(fifth-grade level)

Handicapped

Lasker, Joe *He's My Brother.* The story of a boy with learning disabilities.

McGrath, Edward *An Exceptional View of Life.* Short stories and poems by handicapped children.

Swarthout, Glendon and Kathryn *Whales to See.* A story about a class of children with learning disabilities.

Wolf, Bernard *Anna's Silent World.* A picture book about a deaf girl.

ACTIVITY PAGE

When TV Is Only Part of the Picture

All people are members of different groups, even if they don't think about it. Match up the names of the characters with the groups that they are in, by drawing lines between the characters and the groups. Most characters represent more than one group. Try to use a different color crayon or pencil for each group.

Group	*Character*
Grandparents	Archie Bunker
Teenagers	Fonzie
Italian-Americans	Mr. Bradford *(Eight Is Enough)*
Males (men and boys)	Willis *(Diff'rent Strokes)*
White people	Ann Romano *(One Day at a Time)*
Black people	Mork
Females (women and girls)	
	Mindy
Orkans (people from Ork)	
	Rerun *(What's Happening)*
Fathers	Laverne
Mothers	Mrs. Brady

TEN

VIOLENCE AND ACTION ON TV

Have you ever noticed children imitating some of the action they have seen on television? Sometimes this mimicry may involve just make-believe "galloping" on an imaginary horse and "shooting" with pointed fingers at invisible pursuers. Often, however, if the violence they've witnessed is very realistic, children may also imitate punching, kicking, or some Kung Fu movements. Since children can't pull their punches as well as TV actors, they may occasionally hurt their brothers, sisters, and friends, and provoke a real fight. Those children who watch many violent action shows may begin to adopt some of the mannerisms and provocative attitudes of superheroes or police detectives and resort increasingly to fighting with their friends to settle the inevitable disagreements that arise among playmates.

In the past decade a growing number of social scientists, educators, and mental-health specialists have been concerned that the considerable amount of fictional violence (or even news reporting of actual violence) represented on television may have a harmful impact on youthful viewers. With the national consciousness-raising effort produced by the PTA organization and others in the last five years, more and more parents have been alerted to this possibility as well. Such concerns are not exaggerated, we believe. After all, children grow up watching huge amounts of television daily. From network programming they learn about other countries and different commercial products, and they imitate speech patterns, phrases, and songs. Obviously, they are likely to emulate certain types of aggressive actions from the many incidents of violence presented daily on television. The children we questioned (in the study in which these lessons were tested) reported that they often imitated some of the chases from *CHiPs* on their bicycles or some of the fighting tricks they'd seen on *Baretta*. They also indicated that they occasionally got into arguments within the family by imitating attitudes or aggressive actions they'd seen on the TV set.

It would be foolish to attribute all the violence in America to the influence of television. After all, there was plenty of violence in the country well before the introduction of TV or even the movies. But even if television affects just 10 percent of all children by increasing their aggressiveness, it is still influencing many thousands of youngsters. Major TV networks have in fact reduced a good deal of the prime-time violent programming (including shows such as *Police Woman, Baretta, Starsky and Hutch, The Six Million Dollar Man, The Bionic Woman*) but TV films and reruns on many local stations continue to be full of explicit violence, and they are often broadcast at times when children are very likely to be watching.

While we believe the networks and local stations have a responsibility to curb violent programming, the ultimate responsibility for limiting children's exposure to violence on TV rests with parents and other adult caretakers. The purpose of this lesson is to provide suggestions for teaching children that most violence on TV and in movies is not real and should not be imitated. The lesson will focus on explaining to children why violence is not fun, and on discussing other ways besides aggression to resolve the inevitable problems that arise in daily life.

GOALS

The four goals of this lesson are as follows:

- To understand that the violence portrayed on TV is sometimes distorted
  a. Violence isn't as common in the real world as it is in the TV world.
  b. Violence on TV often seems fun or exciting because the consequences of violence are not usually shown on TV.
- To understand that there are other ways of solving problems that are preferable to violent confrontations
- To understand that television programs can be exciting or suspenseful without showing violent scenes
- To develop familiarity with vocabulary words related to physical and verbal aggression

WHAT YOU NEED TO KNOW

Does violent television programming increase the likelihood that children will engage in more fighting and disruptive behavior? For years many parents and even some mental-health specialists believed that watching violence on TV had little effect on children and might even be good for them, since it served to "drain off" some of their aggressive energy. The extensive research conducted by Professors Albert Bandura of Stanford University and Leonard Berkowitz of the University of Wisconsin has demonstrated quite clearly, however, that both children and adults exposed to violence in movies and TV rarely become less aggressive; rather, the evidence is fairly strong that they show *increasing* tendencies to be aggressive.

The studies we've just mentioned were carried out in rather controlled university settings, and some social scientists and television industry representatives have argued that real-life TV viewing may not produce the same results. A very important long-term follow-up study was completed by a group of investigators led by Monroe Lefkowitz and Leonard Eron in an upstate New York county. They found that boys who had been watching a great many violent TV shows at age eight were rated as more aggressive by their friends and neighbors ten years later, when they were eighteen. By careful statistical methods, the researchers showed that other factors (such as a preference by already aggressive children to watch violent programming, family background, or social class) could not explain away this relationship. The results were clear: The heavy viewing of action shows influenced these children toward becoming more aggressive as they grew up.

More recently Leonard Eron, a professor of psychology at the University of Illinois, has been directing a research team repeating this experiment with third- and fifth-grade children in Chicago. His results to date corroborate these earlier ones, except that now girls as well as boys are showing similar effects of viewing heavy violence, a finding explained perhaps by the increased number of tough, fighting women on shows like *Wonder Woman, The Bionic Woman, Charlie's Angels* and *Police Woman.*

A very large-scale study (sponsored by the Columbia Broadcasting Company) was conducted in England by Professor William Belson. Of 1,500 adolescent boys studied, 188 indicated they had engaged in at least ten or more acts of considerable violence in the previous six months. It turned out that the boys' tendencies to engage in serious acts of violence were particularly related to their intensive viewing of action shows on TV. Belson reported that the programs most related to the boys' increased violence were (1) shows depicting people involved in close relationships who attack one another and other persons; (2) Westerns which feature saloon brawls and fistfights; (3) fictional violence shows with very realistic fight scenes; (4) shows that depict violence as a desirable way to serve a good cause; and (5) programs which use violence for no discernible purpose.

At the Yale University Family Television Center we conducted one of the first studies which examined the relationship between TV viewing at home and the behavior in school of children as young as three and four years of age. In one investigation we found that boys and girls from middle-class backgrounds who were the heaviest TV viewers in this sample, and especially those who watched action shows, were more likely to get into fights and disrupt others' games in the nursery school. As in the Eron study, the viewing of action shows more likely caused this aggression and did not simply reflect a viewing preference by already troublesome children. These findings were further confirmed in a subsequent study we carried out with 200 children from blue-collar and lower socioeconomic family backgrounds. When we looked more closely into the family-life patterns of our children through home interviews, we found that those preschoolers who showed the most aggressive behavior over a year's time came from intact, rather conventional families who allowed the *child* to control the TV set and who had few outside interests, relying on heavy TV viewing as a social outlet.

In the project with elementary school children on which the present lessons are based, we also looked at the effects of TV viewing on behavior in school. We had the teachers rate their third, fourth, and fifth graders on a variety of classroom behaviors and personality traits. Although we didn't find a relationship between television viewing and aggression in the classroom, we did find that those children who watched violent programs with fantasy characters, like *Wonder Woman, The Bionic Woman,* and *The Incredible Hulk,* were unhappy in class and had more difficulty in their interpersonal relationships. It seems clear, then, that watching violent programming has a special, often harmful, impact on children.

Since the extensive research of Dean George Gerbner of the Annenberg School of Communications at the University of Pennsylvania has shown that television—even with recent cutbacks in action shows on prime time—continues to portray a great deal of violence, there is serious reason for helping children confront the nature of such action-packed programming. This is even more the case since further research has demonstrated that older children learn more about aggression from viewing than do younger children, who are more sensitive to constructive, prosocial programming. Boys also are more likely to imitate antisocial behavior from aggressive material than girls. In our own study we observed that the fathers who were heavy TV viewers had children who were likely to watch more action shows and spend less time reading. All of these results point again to the key role of parents' monitoring what's on TV and helping children understand violence in the medium.

Children emulate undesirable attitudes as well as behaviors from watching violent TV. Many youngsters don't grasp the cause-effect relations that lead to fights, and they come to believe that violence is a nice, quick way of resolving problems. The pressure on writers to wind up a complex story in a half hour or 60 minutes leads them to resort frequently to a shoot-out or punch-out solution. Producers also believe that such rapid-fire activities as fights and car chases will hold viewers' attention on the screen so that they will notice the commercials which continually interrupt the story. Research suggests that young children do lose track of the reasons for fights or the moral issues involved in stories because of the rapid pace of programs and the interruptions for advertising.

Children also need some help in dealing with the news. Many acts of violence portrayed each night can be frightening to young children. Action and violent scenes are more dramatic visually than the economics of society, and newscasters tend to select the more graphic items for reporting. Our research found that nursery school children who watched the news and action-detective stories, and who were heavy television viewers, tended to be more aggressive in school. Older children may not be as impressionable as these youngsters, but even they (as well as adults) begin to develop false assumptions about the amount of crime and violence that takes place in the world. According to Professor Gerbner, the news does influence our attitudes about danger in the streets.

You can help children understand violence and, in a way, inoculate them against imitation or misunderstanding by pointing out some of the characteristics of action shows. You can call their attention to the way camera techniques and background music intensify excitement. For example, two characters may say to each other, "I've had enough of you," and "I'm sick and tired of you." If the camera zooms in on their faces, and if menacing music and the beat of drums sound in the background, a fight is likely to erupt. Television relies heavily on zooms, close-ups, and pounding music to excite and subtly lead one to the expectation of a battle.

When a fight does erupt on TV, it is very often convincing, especially to most people who have never been in real fights, and, of course, to children. Children often don't realize that actors miss completely when they swing at each other, and that camera angles and sound effects convey the impression of punches. You should explain to your children that these people are actors pretending to fight and they are well-practiced in how to miss each other. After all, most actors are rather vain about their appearance and wouldn't want to end up with split lips, black eyes, or puffy cheeks.

American television doesn't often show the consequences of fighting or shooting. Characters are shot, fall down, and simply disappear from the plot and the screen. It's important to help children see that real aggression doesn't solve a problem so tidily. Indeed, it is just the beginning of a problem, because if a person is hurt, he or she must spend days, weeks, or months recuperating. The aggressor also may hurt himself in hitting someone else. Also, if he shoots a person, he may feel terrible afterward, and almost certainly would be arrested and stand trial, even if the shooting *was* in self-defense. And policemen or detectives rarely resolve conflicts by shooting people. If they do, they usually have to undergo a hearing to justify their resort to firearms. What, too, of the families of persons shot or injured? They may suffer for years as a consequence. It's all not so simple, and children, we believe, need frequent reminders of this in view of the continuous dosage of "easy" violence they get through television.

We've been talking so far of direct aggression, of persons hitting, strangling, or shooting each other, or engaging in destruction of property. There's also a good deal of verbal insult and "put-down" on television. A great deal of humor on situation comedies comes from abusive remarks such as Archie Bunker's references to his son-in-law as "Meathead" and to his wife as "Dingbat." To adults these seem harmless enough because we've learned that such situations are mainly in comedy and few husbands in real life can talk to their wives the way Archie does. Children often don't grasp this, especially since the laugh-track in the background makes such remarks sound funny. They need to see that such remarks can be made *only* in a humorous setting. To repeat many of the remarks heard on TV to other people would most likely hurt them deeply, and even provoke some real-life aggression. Parents can help children realize that we laugh at characters insulting each other on TV precisely because they're getting away with saying things we wouldn't say in real life.

SPECIAL WORDS AND IDEAS FOR CHILDREN TO REVIEW

Action-packed—a TV program where a lot of things happen in a short time
Aggression (**in context of this lesson**)—saying or doing threatening things without actually becoming violent
Verbal—spoken words
Bloodshed—when people are hurt or killed in violent situations
Violence—acts of cruelty involving physical pain or damage to people or property

DISCUSSION IDEAS

Action shows are shows which portray a lot of activity, such as car chases, fights, or people running to catch someone or to escape from someone. What action shows do you watch?

Read your child this violent passage from a TV script:

An old blue car pulls sharply away from the curb with its brakes screeching, while someone jumps into the passenger seat and slams the door. The car quickly turns the corner and speeds away.

A man starts his motorcycle on another street and begins to weave in and out of traffic. The blue car then pulls into an alley at high speed. The motorcycle turns into the same alley from the other direction. The blue car swerves as the motorcycle falls and skids into some trash cans. The blue car then speeds away.

The motorcyclist gets up and pulls out a rifle from his pack, and quickly runs to the end of the alley, bends down on one knee, takes aim, and fires repeatedly at the blue car. The car is hit and immediately bursts into flames and crashes into a store.

Talk about how reading about violence feels different than watching it on TV. The impact of special effects, music, imagination, etc., should be discussed.

Ask your child to think for a minute about how he or she feels when someone is hurt or killed in a TV program. Does it seem real? Stress that violence is not fun or funny. Ask if the real world is like that. Acknowledge that violence exists, but does not permeate the real world to the extent that television would have us believe. Talk about why there are so many violent TV programs.

Do the stars of TV programs ever get badly hurt or killed? Why or why not?

Parents can explain the concept of verbal aggression.

Why is it portrayed as funny? Is it true that "sticks and stones may break my bones, but names will never hurt me"? Are there alternatives to verbal and physical aggression? Talk about how verbal aggression may seem funny on TV, but not in real life.

Sometimes people imitate verbal and physical aggression that they see on TV. Give examples from their own experiences. Ask your child: "Have you ever noticed yourself imitating violence on TV? Why does this happen? What can we do to stop it?"

ACTIVITIES

1. Choose an action show and a cartoon that you usually watch, and keep track of the violent actions on the Physical Aggression Chart (Activity Page).
2. Choose a situation comedy that you usually watch, and keep track of the verbal aggression on the Verbal Aggression Chart (Activity Page).
3. After watching a TV show that seems violent, write down how you feel.
4. How can you tell the difference between violence on the news and violence on action programs?
5. Interview a real police officer. Ask him or her whether police work is as exciting in real life as it is on TV.
6. Draw two pictures where two people are solving a problem: One is violent and the other is not.

SUGGESTED READINGS

Golding, William *Lord of the Files*
Hall, Lynn *Troublemaker*

Hinton, Susan E. *The Outsiders*
Holland, Isabel *Amanda's Choice*
Wojciechowska, Maia Rodman *The Hollywood Kid*

ACTIVITY PAGE

Physical Aggression Chart

Some cartoons and "action programs" show a lot of chasing, fighting, and bloodshed. If you watch a cartoon or action program, rate how much physical aggression was on the program by answering the following questions.

Name of program: _____

1. How many characters were killed on this program?
2. How many characters were physically hurt (but not killed)? _____
3. Were there any crimes committed on this show? ____ If there were, what were they?
4. Were there any car chases? _____
   Were there any car accidents? _____
   Were there any fires? _____
   Were there any other accidents or disasters? _____
   Name them:
5. How was the bad person punished?
6. Did the program make physical aggression seem fun *or* funny *or* exciting? _____
   Did it show that violence hurts people unfairly?
7. Sometimes programs show violence that seems wrong or silly, because it was not necessary. Could the fighting or killing have been avoided by talking? Could the person have been arrested quietly instead of being chased in a car?

_____

_____

_____

ACTIVITY PAGE

Verbal Aggression Chart

Some "action programs" show people saying mean things to each other, even if they don't fight. Some situation comedies show people making fun of each other by calling each other names or saying mean things about each other. These are examples of verbal aggression.

If you watch a program with verbal aggression, rate the program by answering the following questions:

Name of program: ————————————————

1. What kind of verbal aggression was used on this program?
   a. People said mean things to each other, as if they wanted to hurt the other person physically (for example, "I'll knock you down" or "I'd like to hit you.")
   b. People made fun of each other, calling names or using other verbal put-downs.
2. Can you give an example of verbal aggression from this program?

   ————————————————————————————————

   ————————————————————————————————

   ————————————————————————————————

3. Did the program make verbal aggression seem fun or funny or exciting? How?

   ————————————————————————————————

   ————————————————————————————————

   ————————————————————————————————

4. How would you have felt if someone said something like
   that to you or about you?

   _____

   _____

   _____

ACTIVITY PAGE

Different Ways of Solving Problems
FISTFIGHT

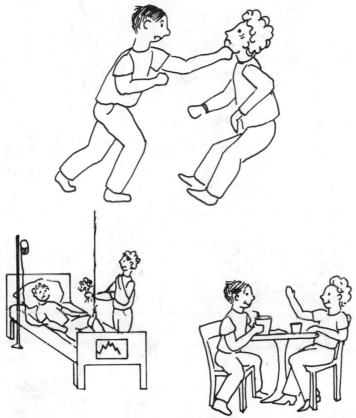

Look at the three pictures on this page. The picture on
top shows two people fighting the way characters on TV
often fight. There are also two pictures on the bottom of
the page. They show what might happen later, after the
fight. Which one of these things do you think would
happen in real life?

GUNFIGHT

Now look at this page. The picture on top shows two men
fighting with guns the way characters on TV often fight.
The two pictures on the bottom show what might happen
later, after the fight. Which one of these things do you
think would happen in real life?

FIGHT OVER TOYS

Here are three pictures again. The picture on top shows
two girls wanting to play with the same toy. The pictures
on the bottom show two things that the girls can do.
Which do you think is the better thing to do?

DIFFERENT WAYS OF SOLVING PROBLEMS

These pictures present children in frustrating situations.
After completing this chapter, look at each picture
separately. Ask your child, "Has something like this ever
happened to you?" "What did you do when this
happened?" "If this hasn't happened to you, what would
you do if it ever did?" "What do you think *this* boy/girl
will do?" "What kinds of things can they say or do to
make things better?"

ELEVEN

COMMERCIALS AND THE TELEVISION BUSINESS

All parents are aware of the powerful influence that television commercials have on their children. For many years TV advertisers have produced commercials that are specifically designed to attract and hold the attention of children of all ages. However, in the last few years there has been increasing controversy regarding whether these commercials are fair, since they are intended to persuade children who are not mature enough to critically evaluate the messages presented. Groups such as Action for Children's Television (ACT) have been especially vocal in their complaints that TV commercials teach children poor nutritional habits and generally encourage the view that having possessions will make a person happy and popular. Perhaps most annoying to parents are commercials' underlying message that parents who love their children will buy them the wonderful products being advertised.

Many parents that we have spoken to express frustration with the persuasive power of TV commercials, and they find it difficult to deal with their children's many requests for food and toys that they've seen advertised. Although research has shown that advertising strongly influences a child's desire for various products, parents can still modify their children's response to commercials. Our experiences with third, fourth, and fifth graders have demonstrated that children can learn to be more critical of television commercials. Although as children mature they tend to become increasingly skeptical about commercials, it is only when they understand the purposes of advertising and the techniques that are used to enhance products that they can critically evaluate what the commercials actually say, what they leave out, and what they subtly imply. Many of the special effects and other television production techniques that were discussed in previous chapters are directly relevant to the understanding of commercials.

GOALS

The four goals of this lesson are as follows:

- To understand why there are commercials on TV
  a. high cost of television productions
  b. sponsor wishes to sell a product to a large market
  c. television networks' desire for profits
  d. to influence attitudes and behaviors
- To develop an understanding of the different kinds of commercials
- To develop the ability to view television commercials critically
  a. What messages are being presented *directly* and what messages are being presented *indirectly?*
  b. What means are typically used to present the message? (technical aspects, distortions)
- To develop vocabulary and language usage pertaining to television advertising

WHAT YOU NEED TO KNOW

The word *commercial* is short for *commercial message.*
Every hour on television is carefully planned to have
enough minutes for these "messages." By selling commercial minutes to advertisers, TV station owners are
able to defray the costs of their productions. It is very
expensive to advertise on television (many thousands of
dollars for every half minute), but commercials are still
a bargain for advertisers, because they only cost about
$8 for every thousand viewers. This is much less expen-
sive than sending a letter to a thousand people, which
would cost $150 for postage alone. So, if an advertiser
wants to reach a large audience, TV advertising costs
less money, and it lets advertisers talk about and visually portray their products.

Children watch an average of 19,000 to 20,000 commercials each year. Most parents assume that their
children understand the purpose of advertising, but
research has shown that youngsters cannot even distinguish between commercials and television programs.
Scott Ward, Daniel Wackman, and Ellen Wartella have
conducted studies of several hundred children in kindergarten, third, and fifth grades. They found that the
majority of the kindergartners did not know what a TV
commercial was, although many were able to describe
the fact that commercials were shorter than programs.
These children did not understand why commercials
were shown on TV or what they were attempting to do.
The third and sixth graders were more knowledgeable,
but even they did not fully understand the purpose of
commercials.

The persuasive power of television commercials was recently demonstrated in a study of preschool children who accompanied their mothers to the supermarket. Psychologists Joann Paley Galst and Mary Alice White found that children who watched more commercial television programs made more requests for purchases while shopping in the supermarket with their mothers. On the average the children attempted to influence their mothers' purchases once every two minutes. The most heavily requested products were sugared cereals and candy, which are frequently advertised in commercials directed at children. The children also attempted to influence many of their mothers' other purchases, including dishwashing and laundry detergents. We would not expect children to be particularly interested in these products, so it seems likely that their requests can be attributed to the heavy advertising of detergents on daytime television.

Television commercials may also encourage a materialistic attitude. In a study conducted by Marvin Goldberg and Gerald Gorn, of McGill University, four- and five-year-old children were asked whether they would prefer to play with a "not so nice" boy who has a toy barn or a "nice" boy who does not have the toy. Children who had seen the toy advertised were twice as likely to prefer to play with the "not so nice" boy who had the toy.

Many commercials hint that a product will make a person happier or more popular. In a study by Bruce Shaak and his colleagues, second and fifth graders were shown a commercial for cookies. In one version of the commercial, a child was shown winning new friends by dispensing the cookies; in the other version the child did not win new friends. Children who saw the commercial where the child gained new friends were more likely to show an increased preference for the cookies. This commercial was especially persuasive for the fifth graders.

The Federal Trade Commission (FTC) is the government agency that is responsible for regulating television commercials. During the last few years the FTC has been actively involved in the controversy about TV advertising directed at children. Action for Children's Television (ACT), a public interest group, has petitioned the FTC to regulate these commercials more effectively, especially those for candy and other sugared products. In 1978 the FTC stated that it is "unfair and deceptive" to address commercials for any product to children who are too young to understand the selling purpose of commercials. In 1979, ACT demanded that commercials be banned from children's television programs. The networks have claimed that this would make children's television programs financially impossible. This debate has continued. However, even if commercials were banned from children's television programs, children would still be exposed to many commercials during their after-school and prime-time television viewing.

In Chapter 6 we talked about some of the effects that are used on TV to make things look better than they really are. Many of those same effects are used in commercials. For example, if you look closely at a pizza commercial, you can see how the light shines on the sauce and cheese, making it look moist and chewy. Advertisers sometimes use slow motion to make the melted cheese drip slowly off the knife. It looks so good you can almost taste it. And that's the idea the commercial is trying to present—the viewer will remember that image when he or she sees the product at the supermarket, and will probably want to buy it.

There are other camera and lighting effects that commercials can use. For example, toys are sometimes held close to the camera with no children nearby, which makes the product seem bigger than it really is. Special lighting, music, and sound effects can also be used to make toys seem more attractive. Editing can also be used to make advertised products seem more exciting. For example, a commercial for a toy rocket might edit together tapes of children looking excited and happy with a tape of the rocket going into space.

When children watch commercials on TV, it's important for them to remember that these ads have one purpose: They want the viewer to buy something. Help your child to see how the advertisers hint at other ideas in order to persuade them to buy. For example, commercials for candy or food may show people eating and having fun with friends. When children (and adults) see these commercials, it seems as though the product being advertised is fun to eat.

Sometimes commercials use television characters or celebrities to endorse the product being advertised. Celebrities are banned from children's commercials, but children may be influenced by celebrities in other commercials. Research by Andrew Iskoe has shown that these celebrities are very effective in persuading children to desire a product. In Iskoe's study of first,

third, and fifth graders, popular celebrities increased
children's preferences for the product advertised up to
67 percent. When commercials like this appear on TV,
parents should talk to their children about the implica-
tions involved. For example, when Dorothy Hamill, the
famous ice skater, advertises a shampoo, children
should understand that the use of this product will not
make them as beautiful or graceful. Or when commercials advertise medicine by filming the scene in front
of the Capitol in Washington, D.C., children should
realize that the U. S. government is not endorsing the
product. Of course, these commercials are not *overtly*
stating these misrepresentations, but they certainly are
hinting at them.

It's against the law to tell a lie on a commercial,
and there are rules that advertisers must follow. For
example, in recent years bread and cereal commercials which promise that their products build muscles
or improve athletic ability have been banned. But
hints are often legal, and may be very effective. Another example can be found in toy commercials.
Here, several toys are often advertised at the same
time. The National Association of Broadcasters'
Codes require that written or spoken disclaimers say
"Each sold separately," but not all children understand that this means each toy must be bought by itself. Parents need to explain to their children that
buying all these toys can add up to a lot of money,
even if each toy is relatively inexpensive. Other disclaimers that may not be understood by children are
"Assembly required" and "Batteries not included."
However, if the disclaimers are worded more simply

(for example, "You will have to buy the batteries yourself") young children are much more likely to understand the message.

Children should also learn about *political advertisements,* since they see them every year at election time. Explain to your child that these advertisements try to get the viewers to vote for someone, instead of telling them to buy something. Point out how these commercials may use some of the same effects that are used to advertise products. For example, if a commercial shows a crowd of people cheering for the candidate, that makes us think that many people are voting for the candidate and so we should, too.

There are other short messages on TV besides commercials, called *public service announcements.* As a special service to the people watching, these announcements are intended to tell them something important. You can point out examples of public service announcements, such as those against littering, or those asking us to give money to a charity.

Television stations that show commercials are called *commercial television stations.* Some of the money the stations receive for showing commercials goes to pay for the programs that we see, and the rest of the money goes to the station itself. The more people that watch the programs on a commercial station, the more the advertiser has to pay to show the commercial. That means more money for the commercial station. Since the commercial station can make more money from a program that more people watch, only the most popular programs will stay on the air.

There's another kind of TV station called a *public*

television station. The money for their programs comes from the government and from donations made by the viewers. There are no commercials on public television, although sometimes after a program, the station asks viewers for contributions. *The Electric Company, Mister Rogers' Neighborhood,* and *Sesame Street* are popular children's programs on public television.

The most important point is to teach your children that commercials tell people to buy what the advertiser is selling, and that showing commercials brings money for programs and additional money for commercial TV stations. Help your children to be aware of what the advertiser wants them to buy and to decide for themselves if it's something they really want or need. Encourage them to think about the actual merits of the product, and to look for ways that effects are used to make things look bigger than they really are, or better, or more fun.

SPECIAL WORDS AND IDEAS FOR CHILDREN TO REVIEW

Advertise—to make a product known to people so that they will want to buy the product

Advertisement—preparing a product to be advertised on TV in a way that will make it look better than any other product of the same type

Brand loyalty—when a person keeps buying a product because of the brand name

Commercials—advertisements on TV. Commercials help pay for the TV programs.

Market—the people that a network or local TV station can reach with its broadcast signal who might buy a product that is advertised

Profit—a profit is the money made when a product is sold for a higher price than it cost to make. Networks and local TV stations make profits by selling broadcast time to sponsors for more money than the TV program cost to make.

Product—the item that is being advertised on a TV commercial

Selling time—Networks and local TV stations sell time (usually 10, 30, or 60 seconds) to advertisers in order to pay for the cost of TV programs. The cost of buying commercial time depends upon the size of program audience and how much time the advertiser wants to buy.

Sponsor—A sponsor helps pay for the cost of a TV program so that it can advertise its product during the broadcast.

DISCUSSION IDEAS

Ask your child if he or she ever bought anything because it looked good on TV. How was it different than was expected? Was that fair? What can we do about it?

Go over the four types of advertisements, using the table below. (Ages eight to twelve)

1. *Commercials:* These advertisements pay for the programs, which cost a lot of money to make. Commercials can try to sell any kind of product.
2. *Political advertisements:* These talk about a person running for an elective office and try to convince people to vote for him or her. The candidate pays the network for the time, so these also help pay for the TV programs.
3. *Promotional advertisements:* A network or station will advertise programs in order to attract a larger audience.

Programs that are popular can charge more for commercial time.

4. *Public service announcements (PSA):* The government tells the networks that they must show these announcements for free. A PSA will give information or try to change people's ideas and behaviors. Examples include antilitter or antismoking messages.

Using the chart below, go over the techniques used in advertising to make products seem better than they really are. (Ages seven to twelve)

Advertising Techniques	Advertising Effects
1. Close-up	makes product look larger
2. Sound effects	makes product seem more fun or exciting
3. Special lighting	makes the product look more attractive
4. Including additional toys or accessories	makes the product seem more fun or exciting
5. Product shown with happy people	makes it look as though everyone enjoys the product
6. Music or songs	helps you remember the product
7. Attractive people using product	makes it seem as if using the product makes you attractive or popular
8. Celebrity talks about product	makes it seem as if using the product makes you attractive or popular
9. Toy shown without any people nearby	makes product look larger

10. Written information such as "batteries not included"   makes the message seem less important if announcer does not also give the same information

ACTIVITIES

1. While watching TV during the weekend, use a chart like the ones below to keep a record of the number of commercials or amount of time used by commercials. (All ages)

    a. How many TV commercials do you watch every day? Next time you watch TV, keep track of the number of commercials for a half-hour program (or for half of an hour program), by writing the name of each product that is advertised. (Also list commercials for political candidates).
    Name of program: _____
    Time that program begins: _____

    Name of Product

    1. _____
    2. _____
    3. _____
    4. _____
    5. _____
    6. _____
    7. _____
    8. _____
    9. _____
    10. _____
    11. _____

12. _____
13. _____
14. _____
15. _____
Time that program ends: _____

b. How much time do you spend watching TV commercials? Next time you watch TV, use a watch or a clock with a second hand, and keep track of the number of minutes spent on commercials for a half-hour program (or half of an hour program). Write down the names of each product (or political candidate). It will help you to remember that most commercials are 15 seconds, 30 seconds, or 60 seconds.

Name of program: _____
Time that program begins: _____
List all commercials and length of time for each:

Name of Product	*Length*
_____	___seconds
_____	___seconds
_____	___seconds
_____	___seconds
_____	___seconds
_____	___seconds
_____	___seconds
_____	___seconds
_____	___seconds
_____	___seconds
_____	___seconds

Time that program ends: __ Total: __ seconds= __ minutes

2. Think of one commercial which made you think a product was better than it really was. Talk about the special effects or other techniques that were used. (All ages)

3. Write an advertisement about a product that would be hard to sell, that people usually would not be interested in buying, e.g., a shoe box, an empty bottle, a balloon. (All ages) a. Draw or paint illustrations to go with it. b. Act it out.
4. List the products on TV commercials which are related to beautifying people, e.g., makeup, shampoos, toothpaste, applicances. Which commercials are exaggerated? Which commercials are "honest" in presentation? (All ages)
5. List the products on TV commercials which are related to eating, e.g., food, drinks, candy. Which commercials are exaggerated? Which commercials are honest? (All ages)
6. List the products which relate to play, i.e., toys and games. Which commercials are exaggerated? Which commercials are honest? How do you know? (All ages)
7. Write down the subject of a public service announcement or political advertisement that you saw on TV this week. (Ages eight to twelve)
8. Turn off the sound while watching a commercial. What did you learn about the product? (Ages seven to twelve)
9. Think of a way to reword or demonstrate one of the following messages so that all children would understand it: "Each sold separately," "Assembly required," "Batteries not included." (Ages eight to twelve)
10. Family Activity: Think of commercials that don't really tell us what a product is like. For example, what does "Coke adds life" tell us about the taste of Coca-Cola?

SUGGESTED READINGS

Research on the Effects of Television Advertising on Children, a report prepared for the National Science

Foundation, is a good review that is recommended for parents.

A pamphlet, *Children's Advertising Guidelines,* is available from the Children's Advertising Review Unit, National Advertising Division, Council of Better Business Bureaus, Inc., 845 Third Avenue, New York, N.Y. 10022.

THINGS TO WATCH FOR IN CHILDREN'S ADVERTISING

1. Is the size of the product made clear?
2. If batteries are needed, is this stated?
3. If assembly is required, does the ad say so?
4. Is a child or adult shown doing something unsafe?
5. Are children shown using a product not intended for children?
6. Are children shown using a product in a way that the average child couldn't?
7. Does the ad suggest that a child will be superior to friends or more popular if he owns a given product?
8. Does the ad employ any demeaning or derogatory social stereotypes?
9. Does the ad suggest that an adult who buys a product for a child is better or more caring than one who does not?
10. Do program hosts or characters appear in commercials within their own programs?
11. In print publications, are the title characters of the publications used in ads within their own publications?
12. If fantasy elements are used, are they clearly "just pretend"?
13. In ads featuring premiums, is the premium offer clearly secondary?
14. Is a child-directed advertising appeal being used for vitamins or medications?

15. Is there anything misleading about the product's benefits?

Prepared by: Children's Advertising Review Unit, National Advertising Division Council of Better Business Bureaus, Inc., 845 Third Avenue, New York, New York 212/754-1353

TWELVE

YOU AND TV: WHO'S IN CHARGE

Throughout this book we've encouraged parents and children to discuss problems with each other, and we've stressed the need for children to become more discerning, active television viewers. We go one step further in this chapter: Here we examine the ways that parents and children can work together to exert *their* influence over network programming. By expressing opinions about programs and commercials, by sending letters to networks, producers, and celebrities, and by being aware of laws and agencies that regulate the industry, viewers can wield their power to bring more appropriate and better quality programming to commercial television.

GOALS

The major goals of this lesson are as follows:

- To become aware of the laws and agencies that influence TV
- To develop an understanding of the viewers' potential influence on TV programming

- To learn to use TV reviews and schedules
- To develop familiarity with vocabulary related to criticism and influence

WHAT YOU NEED TO KNOW

In 1934 under the Federal Communications Act, Congress created the Federal Communications Commission (FCC) to set rules concerning who may broadcast on television and under what circumstances they may do so. Part of the FCC's duties are to allocate available space to public and commercial broadcasters and determine what rights and privileges they may have. The agency also concerns itself with cable television, pay television, and any other communication service. Television stations receive licenses from the FCC which must be renewed every three years. To maintain their licenses, stations must schedule news and community-affairs shows as well as entertainment programs. At least 90 days before its license expires, a station must file an application for renewal with the FCC. This application must include all the information concerning the station's past programming and future plans. The public can inspect this application at the station or at the Washington office of the FCC.

In 1974 the FCC adopted its Children's Television Report and Policy Statement establishing children's programming and advertising guidelines and standards for commercial television broadcasters. This statement emerged after a three-year rule-making proceeding that was influenced by public opinion and pressure groups composed of concerned parents and educators. The guidelines for programming dealt with three main issues: the need for diversified programs that are educational and cultural; the need for specific programming —particularly educational—geared to preschoolers and to school-aged children; and the need for a better-balanced scheduling of children's programs throughout the week, not just on Saturday morning.

The guidelines for advertising that were set forth in this statement specified that advertising in children's programs should be reduced to 9½ minutes per hour on weekdays, that separations between program content and commercial messages should be clear, that "host selling" of products (characters on a program promoting products) should be eliminated, and that "tie-ins" (where products are promoted within the body of the program) should be eliminated.

In October 1979 *A Report of the Children's Television Task Force* was issued to the FCC and made available to the general public. Briefly, the report stated that in the last ten years, very little new children's programming had been produced either for preschoolers or for the older children on public television. The report also noted that few local commercial stations have been willing to produce their own shows, and it concluded that broadcasters had not adequately met the guidelines of the 1974 Policy Statement. In December 1979 the FCC recommended that a certain amount of broadcast time should be set aside for children, specifically 2½ hours for school-age children and 5 hours for preschoolers during weekdays between 8:00 A.M. and 8:00 P.M. This controversy over regulation, which involves the issues of free speech and freedom of the press, has been going on since the beginning of broadcasting.

Another government agency which regulates television, the Federal Trade Commission (FTC), serves to prohibit unfair and deceptive advertising on television. (As we mentioned in the previous chapter, there are also two independent organizations, the Children's Advertising Review Unit of the Better Business Bureau, and the National Association of Broadcasters, which have prepared guidelines for advertisers of products directed to children.) The main difficulty with both the FCC and FTC is their relative inability to enforce regulations. Rarely is a license revoked once it is granted, and only recently have dramatic cases challenging television content come before the courts. One example was the case of fifteen-year-old Ronny Zamora, who killed an elderly woman in Florida. His attorney pleaded "involuntary television intoxication," and the family attempted to sue the three major networks, claiming that Ronny imitated negative behavior depicted on TV. The U.S. District Court in southern Florida dismissed the motion because no specific television program was cited as the stimulus for Ronny's robbery and murder of his victim. Before this famous trial, a nine-year-old girl, Olivia Niemi, was sexually assaulted in California by four youths. The child's lawyer claimed that the assailants got their idea from *Born Innocent,* a graphic TV program aired three days before the assault on Olivia. The courts dismissed the case on the grounds that NBC's right to broadcast was protected by the First Amendment, and that there was no intent to incite violence. The network defended itself by stating that the program was a serious drama depicting some of the problems that take place in a girls' reformatory.

Even before such controversial and violent programs made headlines, public-interest groups had been active in influencing the networks and advertisers to produce better-quality programs and reduce the amount of violence portrayed—especially in programs directed to children. For example, Action for Children's Television (ACT) is continuously waging a campaign for quality programming as well as curtailment of advertising in children's programs. This group has succeeded in eliminating candy-vitamin advertising and has helped reduce violence on Saturday morning cartoon shows. A similar organization, the New York Council on Children's Television, has conducted conferences, workshops, and informal discussion groups to help parents encourage their children to become more selective, to urge parents and children to discuss programs together, and to help parents monitor their children's viewing.

The National Citizens Committee for Broadcasting (NCCB), headed by Ralph Nader, distributes information concerning public television rights and methods for legislation. The NCCB provides a *violence index* which informs the public of programs that have a high incidence of violence, and names the sponsors of these shows. In addition the National Citizens Communications Lobby (NCCL) keeps Congress abreast of the effects of television on the public. In response to public opinion, for example, the Supreme Court has ruled that stations cannot broadcast certain obscene words, especially when children might be part of the audience.

The Council on Children, Media and Merchandising, formed in 1970, has become a watchdog for the public concerning commercials, especially those directed toward the children's market. One of their major concerns is the number of nutritionally poor foods advertised on television, such as candy, cookies, and sugar-cereals. This organization has taken a strong stand urging the Federal Trade Commission to be stricter regarding the enforcement of existing advertising codes involving children's programs.

It is important for children to know that TV programs are responsive to complaints and praise from viewers. You should encourage your child to write to producers, networks, the Federal Communications Commission, or managers of TV stations. Similarly, children should be urged to write to the FTC and to advertisers if they feel a particular commercial is unfair. Parents and children should also be aware of unsuitable scheduling practices. Many times an excellent children's program does not gain a large audience because stations broadcast those shows at times that conflict with a child's schedule. For example, the afternoon specials usually are planned for four o'clock, a time when many children are taking music lessons, playing with friends, attending school club meetings, or participating in sports. Other quality children's programs are scheduled early in the morning, at dinner time, or on Saturday afternoon, when children have other activities planned. You can help your child write a letter about these and other concerns. Some useful addresses are listed at the end of this chapter.

Parents can work together in a variety of ways to

influence networks to broadcast more educational programming as well as programs geared to specific age groups. With other parents and groups such as a local ACT chapter, you can survey your community to find resources that will be useful. The Parent Teacher Association, church groups, Girl Scouts, Boy Scouts, and education associations such as the National Education Association, the American Association of School Administrators, and the National Association of Elementary School Principals have all been interested in the effect of television on youth. With support from these organizations it might be possible to induce a local station to try out new programs that have appeared around the country. Keep informed through your newspaper or magazines about new children's programs. Urge your local station manager to at least investigate the possibility of a trial period. Help publicize good programs by letting other parents know of their existence. Unfortunately, not all people use a guide or newspaper listing to select their daily programs and instead just turn on the set, not knowing what is on.

Support the growth of public television in your community. These stations have been in existence since 1952 and are funded by the Corporation for Public Broadcasting and by annual membership fees. They have no advertising and can offer more specialized programs designed to reach children, the elderly, different ethnic groups, and people with special needs, such as the handicapped. There are public television stations in all states except Wyoming and Montana.

Instructional Television (ITV) broadcasts are programs carried on public broadcasting stations designed to reach children in their schoolrooms. These educational programs are broadcast during school hours and cover a range of subjects. You might want to suggest that your school take advantage of these offerings. Each program is accompanied by written material for the teacher to use with the children to help enrich existing courses.

You might also suggest to your school librarian ways in which television can be linked to books. We list here some ideas:

- *A television bulletin board*—notices of future television programs having educational or positive social messages. Along with the notices, list related books. For pleasure-reading about television, post cartoons with captions. Make a cartoon scrapbook for children, filled with TV-related and book-related cartoons.
- *A "TV-tie-in table"*—Display books that relate to current or recent TV programs such as *Roots, Little House on the Prairie, Little Women, The Hardy Boys, Nancy Drew, I, Claudius* (for advanced readers), and books on *Holocaust.*
- *Books related to TV events*—Use attractive signs to show where a child can find materials related to sports events. Olympics and Super Bowl or World Series games should create an interest in the collection of fiction and nonfiction sports books.

  Feature science books—watch the new science series on public television (such as *3-2-1 Contact*), post notices, and display books on science and biographies of famous scientists.

  Books about outer space, science fiction, and astronomy tie in with programs such as *Star Trek*, and *Battlestar Galactica.*

  The *Big Blue Marble* program could be tied in with books about other cultures and countries. Watch newspa-

per listings for features on cultures around the world.
- *Books about TV*—Set up a special shelf of books describing the television industry, technical aspects of TV, and careers in television. This is a growing field for women.
- *Conversation hour*—Invite parents and children for afternoon or evening discussions comparing books to TV adaptations. Compare settings, characters, endings, etc. Which version is better—TV or the book? Lots of discussion should take place if the notices about the Conversation Hour include the time of the TV program, and if the books are made available for the participants to read before the discussion.
- *TV newsletters as part of library news*—circulate to children—let them know about library books that relate to TV. This could be a one-page newsletter to be sent home for parents to read, too. Have students submit TV reviews.

If you now review your child's TV viewing record (suggested in Chapter 4), and find that your child is not only watching too much TV, but is watching indiscriminately, there are some things you can do to remedy the situation. The most important way that children can "control" television is to carefully choose the programs that they watch. Instead of watching whatever is on or watching the same programs every week, they can look at a television guide or newspaper schedules. Show your child how to use these schedules. Encourage him or her to read any reviews or descriptions of programs. Of course, the examples that the parents set are very important. Our own research has shown that the most important influence on children's viewing habits is their parents' television viewing. Parents' viewing influences how much time the children spend watching TV, the types of programs that they watch, and their perception of television's importance in their lives.

Parents and children can discuss whether they have ever watched programs that they didn't really like—programs that weren't entertaining and didn't teach anything. Discuss self-regulation: Do your children watch TV even when they don't like the program? Encourage your child to set up *guidelines* for TV viewing and make a *schedule* for TV watching. We offer a sample parent guide at the end of this chapter.

Perhaps the most important ingredient in your family's television diet will be the *family discussion* period about program content. Our research indicates repeatedly that the parent, the teacher, or a group leader can make a difference in helping children understand a program and learn from it.

SPECIAL WORDS AND IDEAS FOR CHILDREN TO REVIEW

Criticize—to give your opinion of something after you've thought about it very carefully. This includes saying what you like and what you don't like.

Fair—to be aware that there are good and bad things about a person or event

Influence—to affect a person or thing without apparent force or direct authority

Interpret—to explain the meaning of something

Law—the rules of government that tell people what they must do or must not do

Unfair—to say only good *or* bad things, to give only one side of an issue or event

Viewpoints—your ideas about someone or something

DISCUSSION IDEAS

1. What techniques does TV use to influence your feelings about a TV character? A real person? Be sure your child is aware of laugh-tracks, the responses of other characters, camera effects, and special effects.
2. Review the following important points we made in this book about how TV *influences* us:
   - TV can make something look better than it really is, such as a toy on a commercial.
   - TV, through the use of camera techniques and special effects, can make impossible things seem real (for example, The Hulk or Mork).
   - TV can influence how you feel about a character by showing you how other characters respond to him or her.
   - TV can influence our ideas and feelings toward ourselves and people who are different from us.
   - Special effects, music, lighting, camera techniques, laugh-tracks—all are used to help create a mood and affect our emotions.
   - TV can influence us to act in either an aggressive or a cooperative manner.
   - Television, with all of its many programs, is designed mainly to entertain the viewer.
3. Now, what can we do to *influence* TV? Ask your child if he has ever seen a TV program that he thought shouldn't be on TV. Help your child distinguish between programs and commercials that are bad or unfair and those that are uninteresting, possibly because they are intended for a younger or an older audience. Talk about schedules and guidelines for TV watching. What kinds of things could you do instead of watching TV? Make a list of all the activities you could do alone, or as a family.

ACTIVITIES

1. Choose one of the following activities:
   a. While watching a situation comedy, write down how many jokes that are followed by laughter did not seem funny enough to make viewers laugh aloud.
   b. If you were a TV producer and you wanted the viewers to dislike a character, what techniques could you use?
   c. If you were a camera operator for a commercial and you wanted the viewers to like a political candidate, what would you do?
2. Write a letter to a favorite star, or to his or her network, to tell them what you like or don't like about the program.
3. If you have seen a commercial that you think is unfair or fair, write a letter of complaint or praise to the FTC, the advertiser, the network, or Action for Children's Television.
4. If there is a children's program that is scheduled at an unreasonable time, write to the station or network to request a change of schedule.
5. Write a review of a TV program. You might get some ideas from a television guide review.
6. Read the reviews of the programs scheduled for tomorrow and decide which programs you want to watch. Younger children can talk to their parents about their preferences.

PROGRAM RATINGS

Use the Program Rating activity chart. It can be used to encourage children to evaluate the quality of programs that they watch.

Point to the face that shows how much you liked or didn't like a program. Sub-captions underneath each picture should read, from left to right: A favorite program, Liked it very much, Liked it, Didn't like it very much, Didn't like the program at all, Hated the program

1. Did you learn anything from the program?
2. If so, list one or more things you learned.
3. Instead of watching this program, what could you do?

PARENTS' GUIDELINES: TELEVISION AND YOUR CHILDREN

These guidelines were developed by the Illinois Office of Education, and have been endorsed by the PTA.

1. Start early to develop your child's good viewing habits.
2. Encourage planned viewing of specific programs instead of random viewing. Be physically active with little ones between planned programs.
3. Look for children's programs featuring young people in your child's peer group.
4. Make sure TV viewing is not used as a substitute for participating in other activities such as trips to zoos, museums, or the introduction of hobbies.
5. Open up discussion with your children on sensitive TV themes to offer them the opportunity to raise questions which may remain unanswered in the content of these programs.
6. Explain that TV advertising is being paid for by the mak-

ers of the product being shown and that famous people say nice things about products for money.

7. Balance reading and television activities. Children can "follow up" interesting TV programs by checking out the library books from which some of the programs are adapted and by pursuing additional stories by the authors of those specific books.

8. Help children develop a balanced viewing schedule of action, comedy, fine arts, fantasy, sports, etc.

9. Arrange for a proper antenna or distribution system to bring in a signal from a public television station so children will have the chance to have alternative programming.

10. Point out positive examples which show how various ethnic and cultural groups all contribute to making a better society.

11. Show positive examples of women performing competently professionally and at home.

12. Write to local newspapers, local TV stations, networks, the FCC and/or advertisers about programs which include excessive violence.

TELEVISION ORGANIZATIONS, AGENCIES, & NETWORKS

I. Organizations and Groups

Action for Children's Television, 46 Austin Street, Newtonville, Mass. 02160 (617-527-7870). National organization of parents and professionals, working to upgrade television for children and to eliminate commercialism from children's TV. Membership, newsletter, campaigns, research information, film and library facilities.

Children's Advertising Review Unit, National Advertising Division, Council of Better Business Bureaus, Inc., 845 Third Avenue, New York, N.Y. 10022. Reviews and evaluates advertising directed to children under twelve years of age. Publishes their guidelines in a pamphlet for parents.

Citizens Communications Center, 1812 N Street, N.W., Washington, D.C. 20036. Provides legal assistance and advice to citizens interested in taking action in broadcasting area. Publishes annual report.

Council on Children, Media, and Merchandising, 1346 Connecticut Avenue N.W., Washington, D.C. 20036. The Council, created by Robert Choate, is most active in areas relating to nutrition and food advertising to children.

National Association of Broadcasters, 485 Madison Avenue, New York, N. Y. 10022. Established in 1922, this organization provides a Television Information Office, lobbies on behalf of the industry before Congress, initiates broadcasting research, and prepared the NAB Code which sets standards for programs and commercial formats.

Office of Communication, United Church of Christ, 289 Park Ave. S., New York, N.Y. 10010. Dr. Everett Parker has made the Office of Communication a spearhead of legal efforts to improve minority representation in broadcasting. Publishes some materials, gives advice.

II. Government Agencies

For letters about TV programs: Chairman, Federal Communications Commission, Washington, D.C. 20554

For letters about TV commercials: Chairman, Federal Trade Commission, Bureau of Consumer Protection, Washington, D.C. 20580

III. TV Networks

ABC, 1330 Avenue of the Americas, New York, N.Y. 10019 (212-581-7777)

CBS, 51 West 52 Street, New York, N.Y. 10019 (212-765-4321)

NBC, 30 Rockefeller Plaza, New York, N.Y. 10020 (212-664-4444)

PBS, 485 L'Enfant Plaza, S.W., Washington, D.C. (202-488-5000)

SUGGESTED READING

1. Brown, Ray. *Children and Television.* Beverly Hills, Calif.: Sage Publications, 1976.

   Summary of the past 20 years of research in the area of children and television. This book is divided into three parts: (1) children as an audience; (2) influences on a child's viewing behavior; (3) TV's effects on children.

2. Kaye, Evelyn. *The Family Guide to Children's Television.* New York: Random House, Pantheon Books, 1974.

   Written under the guidance of Action for Children's Television, this book gives information concerning the many types of television programming children are viewing; program guidelines established by the FCC; review of the literature on the relationship between violence and TV viewing; the importance of writing letters of both criticism and praise to television stations; and how citizens' groups can place pressure on both the FCC and local TV stations to change programming.

3. Melody, William. *Children's TV.* New Haven, Conn.: Yale University Press, 1973.

   Commissioned by Action for Children's Television, this book examines the economic aspects of children's television. It suggests that as long as advertisers control programming, children's television will respond only to the advertiser's vested interest and not to the needs of the child. This book explores alternative modes of financing children's television to provide better quality programming without causing financial hardship to the broadcast industry.

4. Potter, Rosemary Lee. *New Season: The Positive Use of Commercial Television with Children.* Columbus, Ohio: Charles E. Merrill Publishing Company, 1976.

Suggests how commercial television may be used to help children acquire better reading and imaginative skills. Reports successful research attempts in these areas.

5. *Window Dressing on the Set: Women and Minorities in Television.*
A Report of the U.S. Commission on Civil Rights, August 1977.

This report discusses television's portrayal of women, blacks, and other minority groups in the 1950's, 1960's, and 1970's. It also discusses FCC rules and regulations concerning these issues.

6. Winn, Marie. *The Plug-In Drug.* New York: The Viking Press, 1977.

Discusses television's potential dangers to children, including: poor verbal skills, inability to concentrate, less interest in reading. Suggestions concerning what can be done to control children's viewing.

APPENDIX

SOURCES FOR TELEVISION-RELATED MATERIALS

A sampling of the wide variety of efforts that is being made to harness the educational potential of television is presented below.

CRITICAL VIEWING SKILLS CURRICULA

A series of curricula have been developed which are intended to help children better understand the be-hind-the-scenes aspects of television productions:

Critical Television Viewing Skills Curriculum (K–5)
Southwest Educational Development Laboratory
211 East 7th Street
Austin, Tex. 78701

The Television Criti-Kit (Middle School)
WNET/Thirteen
Critical Viewing Skills Project
356 West 56th Street
New York, N.Y. 10019

Getting the Most Out of Television
An elementary school curriculum, with

seven videotapes, teacher's manual, and student work-books, developed at
The Yale University Family Television
Research and Consultation Center
405 Temple Street
New Haven, Conn. 06511

READING SKILLS

Several programs have been instituted which provide teacher/parent guides and reading lessons based on scripts from television shows and classic movies:

CBS Reading Program
51 West 52nd Street
New York, N.Y. 10019

Channel: Critical Reading/TV Viewing Skills
Educational Activities, Inc.
Freeport, N.Y. 11520

Movie Scriptreader Program
Films Incorporated
Moviestrip Division
1144 Wilmette Avenue
Wilmette, Ill. 60091

The Television Reading Program
Capital Cities Communications, Inc.
4100 City Line Avenue
Philadelphia, Pa. 19131

PERIODICALS

Prime Time and *Teachers Guides to Television* are two leading periodicals published as viewing guides. Geared to network specials, each presents ideas and activities that teachers and parents can use to help junior high and high school students increase their knowledge of the subject matter shown. *Highlights Magazine* publishes a newsletter featuring a monthly column which suggests how parents can control and use television more actively. Magazines for children, such as *Cricket* and *Scholastic,* frequently have features relating to television.

Prime Time School Television
Suite 810
120 S. LaSalle Street
Chicago, Ill. 60603

Teachers Guides to Television
P.O. Box 564 Lenox Hill Station
New York, N.Y. 10021

INSTRUCTIONAL TELEVISION

The Agency for Instructional Television, a consortium of 19 state and provincial agencies, assists education through the development of television programs which are designed to promote essential critical-reasoning and study skills. The Appalachia Educational Laboratory of West Virginia has developed guides to supplement television shows for preschoolers, such as *Mister*

Rogers' Neighborhood and *Captain Kangaroo.*

Agency for Instructional Television
Box A
Bloomington, Ind. 47401

Division of Early Childhood
Appalachia Educational Laboratory, Inc.
Charleston, W. Va. 25325

INTERACTIVE TELEVISION

Vice Versa Vision, developed in Connecticut, is a project which enables children to actively participate with television characters. *Qube,* a cable project of the Warner Cable Co. piloted in Ohio, permits families to respond to a program host by pushing buttons on their set. Using such systems, students could interact with teachers as if they were face-to-face in the classroom.

ViceVersaVision
Early Learning Center, Inc.
12 Gary Road
Stamford, Conn. 06903

Qube
P.O. Box 2553
Columbus, Ohio 43216

REFERENCES

Throughout this book references are made to research carried out under the auspices of the Yale Family Television Research and Consultation Center. The following is a list of articles and books which specifically describe the design and results of these experiments:

Caldeira, J., J. L. Singer, and D. G. Singer. "Imaginary Playmates: Some Relationships to Preschoolers' Spontaneous Play, Language and Television-Viewing." Paper presented at the meeting of the Eastern Psychological Association, Washington, D. C., March 1978.

Singer, D. G. "Television and Imaginative Play." *Journal of Mental Imagery,* Vol. II (1978), pp. 145–164.

Singer, D.G. "Television Tie-Ins in the School Library." *School Library Journal,* Vol. XXVI, No. 1 (1979), pp. 51–52.

Singer, D. G. "The Constructive Uses of Television in the Classroom." Proceedings of *International Year of the Child, Child Advocacy Conference 1979,* Yale University Child Study Center, New Haven, Conn., 1980.

Singer, D. G., J. Caldeira, and J. L. Singer. "The Effects of Television Viewing and Predisposition to Imagination on the Language of Preschool Children." Paper presented at the meeting of the Eastern Psychological Association, Boston, Mass., April 1977.

Singer, D. G., and J. L. Singer. "Family Television Viewing Habits and the Spontaneous Play of Preschool Children." *American Journal of Orthopsychiatry*, Vol. XLVI (1976), pp. 496–502.

Singer, D. G., D. M. Zuckerman, and J. L. Singer. "Teaching Elementary School Children Critical Television Viewing Skills: An Evaluation." *Journal of Communication*, Vol. XXX, No. 3 (1980), pp. 84–93.

Singer, J. L. "The Power and Limitations of Television: A Cognitive-Affective Analysis." In P. Tannenbaum, ed., *Television and Entertainment. Report of an SSRC Conference.* Hillsdale, N.J.: Erlbaum, 1980.

Singer, J. L., and D. G. Singer. "Television: A Member of the Family." *The National Elementary School Principal*, Vol. LVI, No. 3 (1977), pp. 50–53.

Singer, J. L., and D. G. Singer. "Television-Viewing, Family Style and Aggressive Behavior in Preschool Children." In M. Green, ed., *Violence in the Family: Psychiatric, Sociological and Historical Perspectives.* Washington, D.C.: American Association for the Advancement of Science Symposium Series, 1980.

Singer, J. L., and D. G. Singer. "Television and Reading in the Development of Imagination." *Children's Literature*, Summer 1981.

Singer, J. L., and D. G. Singer. *Television, Imagination*

and Aggression: A Study of Preschoolers. Hillsdale, N.J.: Erlbaum, 1980.

Tower, R. B., D. G. Singer, J. L. Singer, and A. Biggs. "Differential Effects of Television Programming on Preschoolers' Cognition, Imagination, and Social Play." *American Journal of Orthopsychiatry,* Vol. XLIX (1979), pp. 265–281.

Zuckerman, D. M., D. G. Singer, and J. L. Singer. "Television Viewing and Children's Reading and Related Classroom Behavior." *Journal of Communication,* Vol. XXX, No. 1 (1980), pp. 166–174.

Zuckerman, D. M., D. G. Singer, and J. L. Singer. "Children's Television Viewing, Racial and Sex-Role Attitudes." *Journal of Applied Social Psychology,* in press.

Chapter 1

Collins, W. A. "Children's Comprehension of Television Content." In E. Wartella, ed., *Development of Children's Communicative Behavior.* Beverly Hills, Calif.: Sage, 1979.

Cook, T. D., H. Appleton, R. F. Conner, A. Shaffer, G. Tamkin, and S. J. Weber. *"Sesame Street" Revisited.* New York: Russell Sage Foundation, 1975.

Essa, E. L. "The Impact of Television on Mother-Child Interaction and Play." Doctoral dissertation, Utah State University, 1977. *Dissertation Abstracts International,* Vol. XXXIX (1978), 2568B (University Microfilms No. 78–21, 124).

Fink, R. "The Role of Imaginative Play in Cognitive Development." In M. K. Paulsen, J. F. Magary, and G.

I. Lubin, eds., *Piagetian Theory and the Helping Professions.* Los Angeles: University of Southern California Press, 1976.

Golomb, C. "Pretense Play: A Cognitive Perspective." Wheelock College Symposium on Symbolization and the Young Child, 1976.

Harrison, L. F. "The Relationship between Television Viewing and School Children's Performance Measures of Ideational Fluency and Intelligence: A Field Study." Doctoral dissertation, The University of British Columbia, 1977. *Dissertation Abstracts International,* Vol. XXXIX (1979), 412B.

Hornik, R. C. "Television Access and the Slowing of Cognitive Growth." *American Educational Research Journal,* Vol. XV (1978), pp. 1–15.

Piaget, J. *Play, Dreams and Imitation in Childhood.* New York: Norton, 1962.

Rubin, K. H. "The Play Behaviors of Young Children." *Young Children,* Vol. XXXII (1977), pp. 16–24.

Susman, E. J. "Visual and Verbal Attributes of Television and Selective Attention in Preschool Children." *Developmental Psychology,* Vol. XIV (1978), pp. 565–566.

Winn, M. *The Plug-In Drug.* New York: Viking Press, 1977.

Witelson, S. F. "Sex and the Single Hemisphere: Specialization of the Right Hemisphere for Spatial Processing." *Science,* Vol. CXCIII (1976), pp. 425–427.

Chapter 2

Bandura, A. *Aggression: A Social Learning Analysis.* Englewood Cliffs, N.J.: Prentice-Hall, 1973.

Bandura, A., D. Ross, and S. A. Ross. "Imitation of Film-Mediated Aggressive Models." *Journal of Abnormal and Social Psychology,* Vol. LXVI (1963), pp. 3–11.

Belson, W. A. *Television and the Adolescent Boy.* Hampshire, England: Saxon House, 1978.

Eron, L. D. "Sex, Aggression, and Fantasy." Paper presented at the meeting of the Midwestern Psychological Association, Chicago, May 1979.

Friedrich, L. K., and A. H. Stein. "Aggressive and Prosocial Television Programs and the Natural Behavior of Preschool Children." *Monographs of the Society for Research in Child Development,* Vol. XXXVIII, No. 4, Serial No. 151 (1973).

Chapter 4

Dominick, J. R., and B. S. Greenberg. "Mass Media Functions among Low-Income Adolescents." In B. S. Greenberg and B. Dervin, eds., *Use of the Mass Media by Urban Poor.* New York: Praeger, 1970.

Von Feilitzen, C. "The Functions Served by the Media: Report on a Swedish Study." In R. Brown, ed., *Children and Television.* Beverly Hills, Calif.: Sage, 1976.

Frank, R. E., and M. G. Greenberg. "Zooming in on TV Audiences." *Psychology Today,* October 1979, pp. 92–103, 114.

Lyle, J., and H. R. Hoffman. "Television Viewing by

Preschool-Age Children." In R. Brown, ed., *Children and Television*. Beverly Hills, Calif.: Sage, 1976.

Maccoby, E. E. "Why Do Children Watch Television?" *Public Opinion Quarterly*, Vol. XVIII (1954), pp. 239–244.

Mohr, P. J. "Parental Guidance of Children's Viewing of Evening Television Programs." *Journal of Broadcasting*, Vol. XXIII (1979), pp. 213–228.

Murray, J. P. "Television in Inner-City Homes: Viewing Behavior of Young Boys." In E. A. Rubinstein, G. A. Comstock, and J. P. Murray, eds., *Television and Social Behavior* (Vol. 4), *Television in Day-to-Day Life: Patterns of Use*. Washington, D. C.: Government Printing Office, 1972.

Schramm, W. *Men, Messages, and Media: A Look at Human Communications*. New York: Harper & Row, 1973.

Schramm, W., J. Lyle, and E. Parker. *Television in the Lives of Our Children*. Stanford, Calif.: Stanford University Press, 1961.

Stein, A. H., and L. K. Friedrich. "The Effects of Television Content on Young Children." In A. Pick, ed., *Minnesota Symposium on Child Psychology* (Vol. 9). Minneapolis: University of Minnesota Press, 1975.

Tolley, H., Jr. *Children and War: Political Socialization to International Conflict*. New York: Teachers College Press, Columbia University, 1973.

Winnick, M. P., and C. Winnick. *The Television Experience: What Children See*. Beverly Hills, Calif.: Sage Publications, 1979.

Wood, R. W., and C. E. Eicher. *An Investigation of the Television Viewing Habits of Students in Grades Three through Eight in Vermillion, South Dakota.* Vermillion, S. Dak.: University of South Dakota, 1976.

Zill, N. *The National Survey of Children.* Philadelphia: Temple University Institute for Survey Research, 1976.

Chapter 6

Field, M. *Good Company.* London: Longmans Green, 1952.

Huston-Stein, A., and J. C. Wright. "Modeling the Medium: Effects of Formal Properties of Children's Television Programs." Paper presented at the meeting of the Society for Research in Child Development, New Orleans, March 1977.

Salomon, G. *The Language of Media and the Cultivation of Mental Skills.* Chicago: Report of the Spencer Foundation, 1977.

Chapter 7

Garry, R. "Television's Impact on the Child." In *Children on TV: Television's Impact on the Child.* Washington, D.C.: Association for Childhood International, 1967.

Katz, E., and D. Foulkes. "On the Use of the Mass Media As 'Escape': Clarification of a Concept." *Public Opinion Quarterly,* Vol. XXVI (1962), pp. 377–388.

Noble, G. *Children in Front of the Small Screen.* London: Constable, 1975.

Paulson, F. L. "Teaching Cooperation on Television: An Evaluation of Sesame Street Social Goals Program. *A V Communication Review,* Vol. XXII (1974), pp. 229–246.

Piaget, J. *Play, Dreams and Imitation in Childhood.* New York: Norton, 1962.

Snow, R. P. "How Children Interpret TV Violence in Play Contexts." *Journalism Quarterly,* Vol. LI (1974), pp. 13–21.

Stern, S. L. "Television and Creativity: The Effect of Viewing Certain Categories of Commercial Television Broadcasting on the Divergent Thinking Abilities of Intellectually Gifted Elementary Students." Doctoral dissertation, University of Southern California, 1973. *Dissertation Abstracts International,* Vol. XXXIV (1973), 3716A (University Microfilms No. 73–31, 675).

Chapter 8

Edelbrock, C., and A. I. Sugawara. "Acquisition of Sex-Typed Preferences in Preschool-Aged Children." *Developmental Psychology,* Vol. XIV (1978), pp. 614–623.

Erikson, E. *Childhood and Society.* New York: Norton, 1963.

Gorney, R., D. Loye, and G. Steele. "Impact of Dramatized Television Entertainment on Adult Males."

American Journal of Psychiatry, Vol. CXXXIV (1977), pp. 170–174.

Stein, A. H., and L. K. Friedrich. "The Effects of Television Content on Young Children." In A. Pick, ed., *Minnesota Symposium on Child Psychology* (Vol. IX). Minneapolis: University of Minnesota Press, 1975.

Chapter 9

O'Bryant, S. L., and C. R. Corder-Bolz. "The Effects of Television on Children's Stereotyping of Woman's Work Roles." *Journal of Vocational Behavior,* Vol. XII (1978), pp. 233–244.

Chapter 10

Bandura, A. *Aggression: A Social Learning Analysis.* Englewood Cliffs, N.J.: Prentice-Hall, 1973.

Belson, W. A. *Television and the Adolescent Boy.* Hampshire, England: Saxon House, 1978.

Berkowitz, L., ed. *Roots of Aggression.* New York: Atherton Press, 1969.

Eron, L. D. "Sex, Aggression, and Fantasy." Paper presented at the meeting of the Midwestern Psychological Association, Chicago, May 1979.

Gerbner, G. "Measuring the Climate of Fear." *Impact Section, American Medical News,* December 13, 1976, pp. 8–11.

Lefkowitz, M. M., L. D. Eron, L. O. Walder, and L. R. Huesmann. *Growing Up to Be Violent.* New York: Pergamon, 1977.

Chapter 11

Galst, J. P., and M. A. White. "The Unhealthy Persuader: The Reinforcing Value of Television and Children's Purchase-Influencing Attempts at the Supermarket." *Child Development,* Vol. XLVII (1976), pp. 1089–1096.

Goldberg, M. E., and G. J. Gorn. "Children's Reactions to Television Advertising: An Experimental Approach." *Consumer Research,* Vol. I (1974), pp. 69–75.

Iskoe, A. "Advertising via Famous Personalities and the Effects on Children." Unpublished manuscript, The Wharton School, University of Pennsylvania, 1976.

Liebert, D. E., J. N. Sprafkin, R. M. Liebert, and E. A. Rubinstein. "Effects of Television Commercial Disclaimers on the Product Expectations of Children." *Journal of Communication,* Vol. XXVII, No. 1 (1977), pp. 118–124.

Shaak, B., L. Annes, and J. R. Rossiter. "Effects of the Social Success Theme on Children's Product Preference." Paper presented at the Conference on Culture and Communications, Philadelphia, March 1975.

Ward, S., D. B. Wackman, and E. Wartella. *Children Learning to Buy: The Development of Consumer Information Processing Skills.* Beverly Hills, Calif.: Sage, 1976.

INDEX

ABC, 186
Action, 74, 75, 135–55. *See also* Violence; specific types of shows
Action for Children's Television (ACT), 156, 160, 176, 178, 185
Action-packed, defined, 144
Activities, 34–35
Actors, 68. *See also* Characters
Adolescents. *See* Teen-agers
Adventure shows, 23, 48, 49, 52, 100
Advertise, defined, 164
Advertisement, defined, 164
Advertising. *See* Commercials
Aesthetic appreciation, 92–93
Aggression: defined, 144; nonverbal, 146; verbal 145–6, 149. *See also* Violence
Airwaves, defined, 68
Alcohol, 42
All in the Family (Archie Bunker), 143–44
American Indians, 128
Anger, 114–15
Analogies, 121
Animals, Animals, Animals, 52

Animal shows, 50
Animation, 52, 105
Animism, 9
Antennae, 66, 68
Athletics, 35, 48. *See also* Sports shows
Attention, effects and, 10
Audio, defined, 68

Baby-sitters, 37
Bandura, Albert, 20, 138
Baretta, 29, 136
Battlestar Galactica, 30
Belson, William, 20, 139
Berkowitz, Leonard, 138
Better Business Bureau, 175, 185–86
Bewitched, 82
Big Blue Marble, 179
Bionic Woman, 136, 139, 140
BJ and the Bear, 52
Black Beauty, 116
Blacks, 19, 34, 43, 124–25
Bloodshed, defined, 144
Book-related programs, 49
Books. *See* Reading
Boys, 48, 49–50, 113, 141; and *Mr. Rogers' Neighborhood, Sesame Street,* 12, 23; and right-, left-brain

Boys (*cont'd*)
functioning, 9; and sex
prejudice, 33. *See also*
Males; Violence
Born Innocent, 175
Brady Bunch, The, 99, 123
Brain functioning, right- and
left-, 9
Brand loyalty, 164
Brian's Song, 103
Broadcasting, 66, 68
Brothers and sisters, 37

"Camera effect," 76–77
Camera operators, 67, 68
Cameras, 64, 65, 69
Car chases, 85–86
Carol Burnett and Friends, 54
Cartoons, 19, 35, 39–40, 42, 49,
52, 99–100, 104, 105, 176
Causal sequences, 13
CBS, 186
Celebrities, and commercials,
161–62
Characters, 110–21; defined,
117
Charlie's Angels, 30, 111, 126,
139
Children's programs, 49, 53.
See also Preschoolers;
specific shows
Children's Television Report,
173–74
CHiPs, 29, 52, 136
Chroma-key, 81–82, 86
Citizens Communications
Center, 186
Close-ups, 74, 86. *See also*
Zooming
Cognitive properties, 5–6
Cognitive skills, 21ff., 91

Collins, W. Andrew, 13
Comedy. *See* Situation
comedies
Commercials (advertising), 27,
43, 44–45, 74–75, 156–71,
174ff.; defined, 164;
disclaimers, 162–3, 166;
political advertising, 27,
163, 165; public-service
announcements, 163, 165;
and sex stereotypes, 127
Commercial television stations,
163
Concentration, 53
Constructive possibilities,
18–35
Consumers, 26ff., 44
Cook, Thomas C., 12
Cooperation, 22–23, 24–25, 97,
116
Corder-Bolz, Charles R., 127
Corporation for Public
Broadcasting, 178
Council on Children, Media,
and Merchandising, 177,
186
Creativity, 10, 92–93, 99–100;
special effects and, 75–76
Credits, 67, 68
Crime, 142. *See also* Crime
shows; Violence
Crime shows, 48, 49, 99. *See
also* Detective shows
Criticize, defined, 181
Curricula, viewing-skills,
189–90
Cut, defined, 86

Day-care centers, 21–23, 101–2
Defenses, 90
Delaying capacity, 90

Detective characters, 116–17
Detective shows, 19, 33, 40,
    42, 50, 99, 114, 142
Detergents, 159
Diff'rent Strokes, 34, 125
Directors, 66, 68
Disappearance, 82–83
Dissolve, defined, 86
Docudramas, 103
Documentaries, 49, 55
Dramas, 35, 48ff., 52
Drugs, 42

Eating in front of TV, 38–39
Edelbrook, Craig, 114
Editing, 82–84, 86, 103, 161
Educational programs (and
    instructional TV), 19, 48,
    49, 52–53, 178–79, 191–92
Effects, 73–88
Eicher, Charles E., 51
Eight Is Enough, 123
Einstein, Albert, 89
Eleanor and Franklin, 103
Electric Company, 52, 74, 164
Elementary school, 26–35, 49.
    See also specific types of
    shows
Emergency, 52
Emotional disturbance, 93
Empathy, 91
Engineer, defined, 68
Erikson, Erik, 110
Eron, Leon, 20, 138–39
Escape, 51
Essa, Eva, 10
Ethnic minorities. *See* Blacks;
    Stereotypes
Expressions, defined, 117
Eyes, 36–37

Fables of the Green Forest, 24–25
Fair, defined, 181
Families, 19–20, 34, 95. *See
    also* Parents
Family, 52
Family programs, 123; dramas,
    50
Fantasy, 0, 52; demystification,
    62ff.; and illusion, 73ff., 87,
    103–4; shows, 32ff., 49,
    101. *See also* Pretending;
    Reality; Special effects
Fast motion, 85
Fathers, 30, 33, 141
Fawcett-Majors, Farrah, 111
Federal Communications Act,
    173
Federal Communications
    Commission (FCC),
    173–74, 177, 186
Federal Trade Commission
    (FTC), 160, 175, 177,
    186
Females (women), 43, 48, 49,
    111, 114, 122, 126–27. *See
    also* Girls; Mothers
Fiction, defined, 105
Field, Mary, 75
Fights, 104, 142–43
Fink, Robert, 15
Flintstones, The, 52
Florida, 175
Foresight, 92
Foulkes, David, 100
Frank, Ronald E., 48
Freeze-frame, 87
Freud, Sigmund, 90
Friedrich, Lynette, 20, 98,
    115–16
Friends, 24–25, 34, 37

Galst, Joann Paley, 159
Game shows, 13, 19, 33, 40, 42, 50, 53, 127
Garry, Ralph J., 99
Gerbner, George, 140–41, 142
Gifted children, 100
Girls, 50, 127; and imaginary playmates, 98, 113; and right-, left-brain functioning, 9; and *Sesame Street*, 12; and sex prejudice, 33; and viewing of violence, 139. *See also* Females
Goldberg, Marvin, 159
Golomb, Claire, 15
Good Morning America, 81
Good Times, 125
Gorn, Gerald, 159
Gorney, Roderic, 116
Government agencies, 186
Greenberg, Marshall G., 48
Guidelines, 184–85
Guilford's test, 99–100
Gulliver's Travels, 104

Hamill, Dorothy, 162
Handicapped persons, 42; books on, 133
Happy Days, 52, 103–4, 116
Harrison, Linda, 10
Headsets, 67
Hobbies, 34–35
Hollywood Squares, 53
Holocaust, 35
Homework, 35, 38
Hornik, Robert, 11, 15
Hot Hero Sandwich, 55, 74
Hyperactivity, 40

Identity, 110–11; defined, 117
Idol, defined, 117

I Dream of Jeannie, 82, 127
I Love Lucy, 33, 127
Imagination (imagery; pretend), 9ff., 15ff., 20ff., 38, 40, 89–109; imaginary playmates, 98, 113; special effects and, 75–76. *See also* Playing
Incredible Hulk, The, 29, 30, 32, 49, 52, 73, 104, 115, 140
Influence, defined, 181
Instructional television. *See* Educational programs
Insults, 143–44
Intelligence (IQ), 32–33
Interactive television, 192
Interpret, defined, 181
Iskee, Andrew, 161–62

Jacques Cousteau, 52–53
Jeffersons, The, 34
Jetsons, The, 33

Katz, Elihu, 100
Knievel, Evel, 40, 114

Language (words), 10, 11, 20, 21, 27–28, 98; accents, 44; insulting, 43–44, 143–44; obscene, 176; offensive; and preoperational thinking, 8–9; and sexual differences, difficulties, 9; vocabulary, 91, 94
Laugh-In, 7, 113
Laverne & Shirley, 52
Law, defined, 181
Leadership, 22
Lefkowitz, Monroe, 138
Left-, right-brain functioning, 9

Lens, camera, 64
Lighting, 37
Lighting directors, 67
Little House on the Prairie, 47, 52
Live, defined, 105
Long shots, 74, 85
Long-term memory, 7
Lower classes (poor children; working class), 15, 19, 21, 94, 140
Loye, David, 116

Maccoby, Eleanor E., 51
Magic, 8
Makeup, 105
Males, 48, 49, 111, 116. *See also* Boys; Fathers
Market, defined, 164–65
Mary Tyler Moore Show, 104
Materialism, 159
Mature programs, 42–43
Meals, in front of TV, 38–39
Meet the Press, 55
Memory, 7, 10
Men. *See* Males
Microphones (mikes), 68
Middle class, 23–24, 100, 139–40; average viewing time, 19; and *Sesame Street,* 12
Mister Rogers' Neighborhood, 11–12, 23, 53, 96–97ff., 116, 164
Modeling behavior, 101–2. *See also* Characters; Roles
Mohr, Phillip, 50
Monitors, 67
Moore, Mary Tyler, 104
Moral development, 24–25
Moral reasoning, 25

Mork & Mindy, 49, 52, 113, 116
Mothers, and soap operas, 40–41
Movies, 48
Music, 34, 35; programs, 49 (*See also* Variety shows)

Nader, Ralph, 176
National Association of Broadcasters, 162, 175, 186
National Citizens Committee for Broadcasting (NCCB), 176
National Citizens Communications Lobby (NCCL), 176
National Society for the Prevention of Violence, 36–37
NBC, 175–76, 187
Networks, 68, 186–87
Newsday, 18–19
News programs, 19, 49, 50, 54–56, 74, 81, 99, 103, 142
New York Council on Children's Television, 176
New York Times Magazine, The, 89
Niemi, Olivia, 175
Noble, Grant, 100
Nonfiction, defined, 105
Nursery schools, 21–24, 96, 140, 142. *See also* Preschoolers
Nutrition. *See* Commercials

O'Bryant, Shirley L., 127
Obscene language, 176
Old people (the elderly), 43, 128

Orange, Conn., 27–35
Organizations, 185–86
Osmond Family, The, 54

Panning, 76, 87
Parents, 15, 21, 35, 94, 98,
100, 101, 110; guidelines
for, 184–85; social
interaction with, 10, 11;
some answers for, 36–45;
special programs to
stimulate discussions with
teen-agers, 26; viewing
habits (when you watch
and what you watch), 30,
46–61. See also specific
topics.
Parent-Teacher Association,
135
Paulson, Leon, 97
PBS, 187
Periodicals, 191
Personality traits, 115
Piaget, Jean, 8, 94
Picture, defined, 68
Planning, 92
Playing, 10ff., 34, 40; benefits
of, 88ff., 94, 98, 122. See
also Imagination;
Pretending
Plug-in Drug, 15
Police, 123–24; shows, 50
Police Woman, 136, 139
Political advertisements, 163
Poor children. See Lower
classes
Popeye, 52
Popeye (movie), 113
Positive emotionality, 22, 90
Prejudice, 128. See also
Stereotypes
Preoperational thought, 8–9

Preschoolers, 21–24, 49, 99,
139–40; and commercials,
159. See also Children's
programs; specific types of
shows
Pretending, 89–109. See also
Imagination
Prime Time, 55
Prime Time School Television,
191 Prime-time
programming, 50
Privacy, 95
Processing of material, 7
Producers, 66, 69
Product, defined, 165
Profit, defined, 165
Programming, 172–88
Props, 67, 105
Public-affairs programs, 50
Public-service announcements,
163
Public television stations,
163–64, 178

Quincy, 30

Race: prejudice, 34;
stereotypes, 124–25
Radio, 14, 95–96
Rape, 41
Ratings, teacher, 30–32
Reading (books), 11, 13–15, 21,
32–33, 34, 38, 47, 49, 101,
179, 180; -skills materials,
190
Reality, 16, 90ff., 122. See also
Fantasy
Rehearse, defined, 69
Religious activities, 35
Report of the Children's
Television Task Force, 174
Right-, left-brain functioning, 9

Teen-agers (*cont'd*)
    to stimulate discussion
    with parents, 26; and
    violence, 139
"Television," origin of word, 63
Television news magazines, 55
Television set, defined, 69
Temple University, 50
Thinking. *See* Imagination
Thirty Minutes, 55
This Is Your Life, 101
3-2-1 Contact, 53
Thunder, 79
Time: selling of, 165; viewing,
    19, 37, 47
Today, 81
Tolley, Howard, 51
Toys, 95. *See also*
    Commercials

Unfair, defined, 181
United Church of Christ, 186

Variety shows, 33, 42, 49, 50, 54
Vega$, 30
Verbal, defined, 144
Video, defined, 69
Videotape, defined, 69
Vietnamese War, 51
Viewpoints, defined, 181
Violence (and aggression), 11,
    13, 19–20, 23, 27ff., 33,
    34–35, 39, 41–42, 49, 75,
    99, 100, 116, 125, 135–55,
    175–76; defined, 144;
    index, 176; TV fights, 104,
    142–43. *See also* specific
    types of shows

Vision, 36–37
Vocabulary, 91, 94
Von Feilitzen, Cecilia, 51

Wackman, Daniel, 158
Waiting behavior, 90
Waltons, The, 53, 116
Ward, Scott, 158
Wartella, Ellen, 158
Westerns, 49, 99, 139
Wheel of Fortune, 53
White, Mary Alice, 159
Williams, Robin, 113
Winn, Marie, 15
Winnick, Charles, 49
Winnick, Mariann, 49
Wipes, 79–80, 81, 87
Wish fulfillment, 51
Witelson, Sandra, 9
Women. *See* Females
Wonder Woman, 32, 73, 139,
    140
Wood, Robert W., 51
Woody Woodpecker, 52
Words. *See* Language
Working class. *See* Lower
    classes
Wright, John, 75

Yale University Family
    Television Research and
    Consultation Center, *x*ff.,
    20ff., 138

Zamora, Ronny, 175
Zooming, 10, 75, 77–79, 87
Zuckerman, Diana M., *ix*ff.,
    195

Road Runner, 9
Rockford Files, The, 30
Roles, 91–92. *See also*
    Characters; Stereotypes
Roots, 35, 125
Rubin, Kenneth, 15

Salomon, Gavriel, 75
Saturday morning, 39–40, 50,
    176
Saturday Night Live, 54
Scene, defined, 69
Scheduling, 37, 177
Schramm, Wilbur, 51
Science fiction, 48, 50, 74
Screen, TV, defined, 69
Script, defined, 69
Script writers, 66, 69
Self-entertainment, 90
Selling time, defined, 165
Serials. *See* Soap operas
Sesame Street, 11–12, 23, 53,
    74, 97, 164
"Sesame Street" Revisited, 12
Set designers, 66
Sets, 66–67
Sexes, 41; and identity,
    110–11. *See also* Females;
    Males; Stereotypes
Shaak, Bruce, 159
Shopping, supermarket, 159
Short-term memory, 7
Shot, defined, 87
Singer, Dorothy G., *ix*ff.,
    193–4
Singer, Jerome L., *ix*ff., 193–4
Sisters and brothers, 37
Situation comedies, 35, 49, 50,
    52, 114, 143–44
Six Million Dollar Man, The,
    32, 52, 73, 79, 104, 136
60 Minutes, 55

Slow motion, 85, 87
Snow, Robert P., 99
Soap operas, 40–41, 53
Social behavior, 10, 11, 21ff.,
    97. *See also* Families;
    Friends; Roles
Sound, defined, 69
Special effects, 10, 73–88; *See
    also* Commercials
Special problems, 42–43
Speech. *See* Language
Split screen, 80, 87
Sponsor, defined, 165
Sports Day, 101
Sports shows, 35, 48, 50, 53, 81
Starsky and Hutch, 30, 116,
    136
Station, TV, defined, 69
Steele, David, 116
Stein, Aletha, 20, 75, 98, 115
Stereotypes, 16, 34, 43, 111ff.,
    122–34; defined, 129
Stern, Stanley L., 100
Studio, defined, 69
Stunts, 40, 105, 114
Sugawara, Alan, 114
Superfriends, 52
Superheroes, 98, 113. *See also*
    Special effects; specific
    shows
Supermarket shopping, 159
Susman, Elizabeth, 10
Swiss Family Robinson, 24–25,
    116
Switcher, 79–81

Talking. *See* Language; Social
    behavior
Talk shows, 49, 53–54, 103
Taped, defined, 105
Teen-agers (adolescents), 48,
    50, 110; special programs